The ECONOMIC RECONSTRUCTION Of LITHUANIA After 1918

The ECONOMIC RECONSTRUCTION Of LITHUANIA After 1918

Anicetas Simutis

NEW YORK : MORNINGSIDE HEIGHTS
COLUMBIA UNIVERSITY PRESS
1942

FOREIGN AGENTS: OXFORD UNIVERSITY PRESS, Humphrey Milford, Amen House, London, E. C. 4, England, and B. I. Building, Nicol Road, Bombay, India

MANUFACTURED IN THE UNITED STATES OF AMERICA

To the Ideals of the

ROOSEVELT-CHURCHILL

ATLANTIC CHARTER

PREFACE

The purpose of this study is to contribute to an understanding of all the phases of economic reconstruction of one of the Baltic republics, Lithuania. The subject assumes greater interest when it is taken into consideration that Lithuania was impoverished during the World War, that even its few small industries had been destroyed during the hostilities, and that Lithuania had no natural resources such as gold, silver, iron, and coal. In the comparatively short period of her independence—twenty-two years—Lithuania improved her agriculture, developed her foreign trade, and made very substantial progress in every branch of her economic life. Before the Soviet Russian occupation in June, 1940, Lithuanian agricultural products reached the farthest corners of the world and were known for their excellent quality. Yet most of the valuable enterprises that enabled Lithuania to participate in the world market did not exist before the World War, when Lithuania was part of Russia.

The author gratefully acknowledges his indebtedness to Dr. Michael T. Florinsky of Columbia University for his generous criticism during the preparation of this volume; to Jonas Budrys, Consul General of Lithuania at New York, for his encouragement and for the use of his library; and to Joseph A. Boley for his courteous assistance in shaping the final form of the manuscript.

Originally this work was completed in 1940 and submitted in partial fulfillment of the requirements for the degree of Master of Arts in the Faculty of Political Science, Columbia University, but since then it has been revised and brought up to date.

ANICETAS SIMUTIS

New York, N.Y.
January, 1942

CONTENTS

TABLES

CHARTS

The ECONOMIC RECONSTRUCTION Of LITHUANIA After 1918

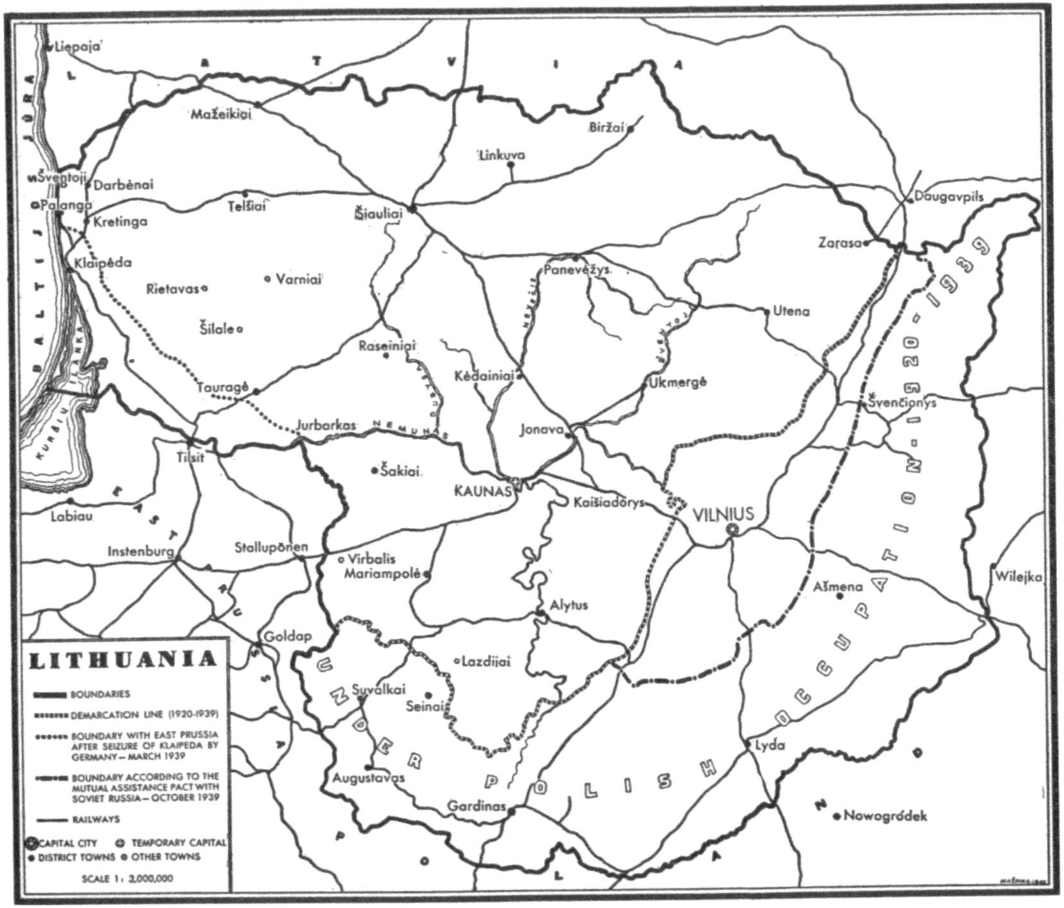

LITHUANIA
BOUNDARIES
DEMARCATION LINE (1920-1939)
BOUNDARY WITH EAST PRUSSIA AFTER SEIZURE OF KLAIPEDA BY GERMANY—MARCH 1939
BOUNDARY ACCORDING TO THE MUTUAL ASSISTANCE PACT WITH SOVIET RUSSIA—OCTOBER 1939
RAILWAYS
CAPITAL CITY
TEMPORARY CAPITAL
DISTRICT TOWNS
OTHER TOWNS
SCALE 1: 3,000,000
LATVIA
BALTIJOS JŪRA
KURŠIU ILANKA
EAST PRUSSIA
POLAND
UNDER POLISH OCCUPATION 1920-1939
NEMUNAS
NEVĖŽIS
DUBYSA
ŠVENTOJI
Liepaja
Mažeikiai
Biržai
Linkuva
Šventoji
Darbėnai
Palanga
Kretinga
Telšiai
Šiauliai
Daugavpils
Zarasa
Klaipėda
Rietavas
Varniai
Panevėžys
Utena
Šilale
Raseiniai
Kėdainiai
Ukmergė
Tauragė
Švenčionys
Jurbarkas
Jonava
Tilsit
Šakiai
KAUNAS
Kaišiadorys
VILNIUS
Labiau
Instenburg
Stallupönen
Virbalis
Mariampolė
Wilejka
Ašmena
Alytus
Goldap
Lazdijai
Suvalkai
Seinai
Lyda
Augustavas
Gardinas
Nowogródek

Chapter I

INTRODUCTION

Lithuania as a nation has a great past. Although it has been definitely established that the country was in existence before the twelfth century, there is a long shadowy period preceding her recorded history.

HISTORIC BACKGROUND

The Lithuanian people form a distinct race and they speak their own language, which is wholly different from the languages of the neighboring countries of Russia, Poland, and Germany. Philologists find the Lithuanian language very helpful for comparative language studies and research, and some of them have found Lithuanian to be very close to the Sanskrit.

The first to mention and describe the people on the Baltic shores was the Roman writer, Tacitus, who at the end of the first century, in his treatise *Germania,* calls them *aestii, aestiorum gentes.*[1]

The Aestii, like most European peoples (Germanic, Slavic, Celtic, Italian, Hellenic), belong to the Indo-European family of nations, although whence the Aestii came to the Baltic shores is still a problem to historians. Philologists find three groups of Aestii: Prussians (Lithuanian *Prusai;* German

[1] A. Sapoka, *Lietuvos Istorija* (History of Lithuania), Svietimo Ministerijos K.L.K. Leidinys, Kaunas, p. 18.

Preussen; Latin *Borusi*), Latvians (Lithuanian *latviai;* German *Letten*), and Lithuanians (Lithuanian *lietuviai;* German *Litauer*). The main distinction among these three groups was that they spoke different dialects of the Lithuanian language.

The Prussians were conquered by the Teutonic Order in the thirteenth century. Castles were built in the conquered regions, and around them German colonists settled. Within fifty years (by 1280) the Prussians had virtually come under German control, although they defended themselves vigorously. In 1243 and again in 1260 there were big uprisings. In the course of years the Prussians were partly exterminated, while those remaining were assimilated and eventually adopted the German language.[2] But as late as the eighteenth century Lithuanian was the dominating language of the population in the region stretching from Königsberg north and east to the Lithuanian-German border.

The Latvians (Letts) were divided into several tribes, namely, Kursiai, Zemgaliai, and Latgaliai. Another, wholly distinct, group called Livs (Latin *Libii*) lived in the basin of the Dauguva. This group belonged to the Ugro-Finnic family of nations, to which the Estonians, Finns, and Hungarians belong. When German merchants and missionaries began to visit the natives of the basin of the Dauguva, they first met the Liv tribes, and thereafter they referred to all of that country as Livonia. In this way the Teutonic Knights of that part of the country came to be known as the Livonian Order (*Fratres Militiae Christi* or Livonian Order of Swordbearers). Despite over six centuries of subjugation to the Germans and later to Russian rule and influence, the

[2] A. E. Ewald, *Die Eroberung Preussens durch den Deutschen* (The Robbery of Prussians by Germans), 1884, Vols. I–IV; M. Oeler, *Geschichte des deutschen Ritter Ordens* (The History of the Teutonic Knights), 1908.

Latvians have preserved their language and their national spirit. After the World War Latvia declared her independence and dropped the name of Livonia.[3]

The Lithuanians are considered to be the main division of the Aestii. They themselves were divided into Zemaiciai (Samogitians), Sudavai, Jotvingiai, and Aukstaiciai (Highlanders). At the end of the twelfth century the Lithuanians began to form a state, because continual wars with the Teutonic Order in the west (Prussia) and in the north (Livonia) forced them to unite. The first crowned king of Lithuania was Mindaugas (Mindow, Mendog), who conquered all the other chieftains, in 1251 adopted Christianity, which had been brought by the Teutonic Knights, and in 1253 was crowned.[4]

At the same time the Samogitians, who continued to fight the Knights of the Livonian Order, succeeded in checking them from making further inroads into the Lithuanian territories. In their effort to conquer the Samogitians, the Teutonic Knights in 1252 built a castle in the vicinity of Klaipeda, to which they gave the German name Memel.

Soon after the death of Mindaugas, Christianity disappeared almost completely in Lithuania.

In the period of 1295–1316 Lithuania was ruled by Vytenis (Witen), who was succeeded by Gediminas (Gedimin), 1316–41. So many Russian territories were incorporated in the latter's state that the new lands greatly exceeded in size ethnographic Lithuania. The title of the ruler in the documents was therefore *Rex Lithuanorum et Multorum Ruthenorum*.[5]

[3] Sapoka, *op. cit.*, p. 42.

[4] J. Totoraitis, *Die Litauer unter dem Koenig Mindowe* (The Lithuanians under King Mindowe), 1905.

[5] Sapoka, *op. cit.*, p. 60.

Gediminas left seven sons, of whom Algirdas (Olgird) was made grand duke of Lithuania, and Kestutis, whose seal bore the inscription *Sigillum Kynstutte Dux de Tracken,* was made grand duke of western Lithuania. They both carried on negotiations with the Teutonic Knights for the Christianizing of Lithuania, imposing as their chief condition that all the territories inhabited by Lithuanian tribes should be returned to them.

Algirdas at the time of his death (1377) appointed as his successor one of his sons, Jogaila (Jagello), who was supposed to rule Lithuania in coöperation with, and on the advice of, his uncle, Kestutis. However, after Kestutis's death Jogaila did not want to grant even any heritage rights to Kestutis's son Vytautas (Witold, Vitovt; his Great Seal was inscribed *Sigillum Alexandri Alias Witowdi Dei Gratia Ducis Lithuaniae*).

In 1384 a delegation of the Polish nobility offered to Jogaila in marriage the hand of the heiress to the Polish crown, Jadwiga, and in 1385 an agreement in the matter was reached. Close collaboration was established between the two sovereign states, Lithuania and Poland, an association from which Poland benefited.

Lithuania reached the peak of her greatness under Vytautas (1392–1430). During his reign, Lithuania extended from the Baltic Sea at Palanga to the Black Sea between the Dnieper and Dniester rivers. In 1410 he successfully led the Lithuanian armies in the battle of Grünwald at Tannenberg, now East Prussia, in which the joint Lithuanian and Polish forces defeated the Teuton, thereby bringing about the collapse of the powerful Teutonic Order. It is to be noted that this battle was led by two great Lithuanians—Vytautas, as grand duke of Lithuania, and his cousin Jogaila (Jagello-Wladislaw), as king of Poland.

Near the end of his reign (1429) Vytautas decided to have himself crowned king of Lithuania. But the Polish noblemen and politicians, wishing to keep Lithuania a grand duchy under the crown of the Polish kingdom, opposed Vytautas's assumption of the crown. The most ardent foes of the creation of a separate kingdom of Lithuania were the Polish clergy under the leadership of Bishop Zbignev Olesnicki. Through the intrigues of Polish politicians the coronation was delayed, and Vytautas died uncrowned on October 27, 1430.

With the death of Vytautas the state began to disintegrate. No one of his successors was capable of ruling that big state so that its harmony and unity would be preserved. Besides, Poles and later Russians knew how to promote dissension among the various peoples residing within its borders.

The Union signed at the Lublin *Seimas* (diet), composed of Polish and Lithuanian representatives, in 1569 was the final act of Lithuania as a separate state. By this agreement a great part of the territory of the grand duchy of Lithuania was given to Poland. The feeling against the Union was intense. Katkewicz, a representative of the grand duchy of Lithuania, with tears in his eyes pleaded with the diet, the Lublin *Seimas,* against the signing of the agreement. The Lithuanian delegates went down on their knees in their entreaty to prevent the action. But in spite of their opposition, the will of the King and the Polish representatives prevailed and the Union was signed.[6]

In the years that followed this unhappy Union, the grand duchy of Lithuania experienced one misfortune after another.

[6] Sapoka, *op. cit.*, p. 226.

Her greatest disaster came in 1795 when, together with Poland, she was partitioned between Russia and Prussia. The greater part of ethnographic Lithuania was given to Russia and the lesser part, to Prussia.

Even though the Lithuanian-Polish state collapsed, the Lithuanian nation continued to exist, although it was badly impaired and its size diminished by more than two thirds.

Lithuanians were under the stern rule of Czarist Russia for 123 years until, on the 16th of February, 1918, the National Council in Vilnius (Vilna) declared Lithuania an independent state, with ancient Vilnius as its capital.[7] On July 12, 1920, during the war between the Soviets and the Poles, Lithuania signed in Moscow with the Soviet government a peace treaty by which the city of Vilnius with the region about it was assigned to Lithuania.[8]

But the old Polish scheme began to manifest itself again. After defeating the Soviet troops near Warsaw, the Poles appeared on the southern Lithuanian frontier and precipitated fighting with the Lithuanians. Finding the going more difficult than they expected, the Poles started negotiations which were carried on under the supervision of the League of Nations and resulted in the conclusion of the Treaty of Suvalkai[9] on October 7, 1920.[10] Two days later, however, the special Polish army, commanded by General Zeligowski, took the Lithuanians completely by surprise and occupied the city of Vilnius and the Vilnius region, comprising almost one third of ethnographic Lithuania. This treacherous act re-

[7] See Appendix A for the text of the Declaration of Independence.

[8] Pranas Dailide, *Lietuvos Sutartys su Svetimomis Valstybemis,* Uzsieniu Reikalu Ministerijos leidinys, Tomas I, 1919–29. Recueil des traites conclus par la Lithuanie avec les pays étrangers, Publie par le Ministère des Affaires Étrangeres. I (1919–29), 30–52. See Appendix B for the extract from the text of the peace treaty with Russia.

[9] Dailide, *op. cit.,* pp. 58–61.

[10] See Appendix C for the text of the Treaty of Suvalkai.

ceived well-merited censure from the League of Nations. Léon Bourgeois, then president of the League, officially referred to this occupation, verbally and in writing to Paderewski, Polish delegate to the League, as "a violation of the undertakings given to the Council." [11] But neither then nor throughout the subsequent years of their country's independent existence did the Polish government once attempt to adjust the grave injustice committed against its neighbor in violation of its own treaty.[12] Instead, the Polish government sought to legalize its *fait accompli* by local elections. In regard to this measure, Hymans, then spokesman for the League of Nations, at the seventh sitting of the Council at Brussels, said:

> In the opinion of the Council, the plebiscite should be taken in conditions of absolute freedom. It should be sincerely and quickly done. But this has become impossible on account of the *coup de force* of General Zeligowski. The League of Nations did not desire a camouflaged plebiscite or the maintenance of these troups in the Vilna region.[13]

But the Polish government managed the elections for the so-called *Vilna Seim* (diet), whose delegates voted an act of incorporation of the Vilnius region into the Polish state. The Council of the League of Nations, however, in its resolutions of January 13, 1922, refused to recognize the legality of the elections conducted under these unfair conditions.[14]

On March 15, 1923, the Conference of Ambassadors put into effect a decision handing over to Poland Vilnius and

[11] *The Vilna Question; Opinion of MM. A. De Lapradelle, Louis le Fur, and Andrew N. Mandelstam concerning the Binding Force of the Decision of Conference of Ambassadors of March 15, 1923.* Authorized Translation from the Original Texts, London, 1929, p. 15.

[12] Lithuanian Information Bureau, *The Vilna Problem,* London, 1922, p. 16. (Hereafter referred to as L.I.B.)

[13] *Ibid.*, p. 17.

[14] *Ibid.*, pp. 24–25.

adjoining districts. This decision, which was met by vehement protests on the part of Lithuania to the League of Nations, was never recognized by the Lithuanian government. According to such an authority on international law as André Mandelstam, the Lithuanian government is not bound by the decision of the Conference of Ambassadors. In his opinion, "The Government of the Lithuanian Republic is not bound, either in law or equity, by the decision of the Conference of Ambassadors of March 15, 1923, regarding the Polish-Lithuanian frontiers." [15]

Thus the Vilnius incident was the first failure of the League of Nations to exact respect for its authority from a recalcitrant member (Poland). This example, which was later followed by other states, poisoned international relations, in the course of years reduced the authority of the League of Nations to the lowest ebb, and finally resulted in the League's complete inability to solve international disputes.

Lithuania, in protest, broke off diplomatic, consular, political, and economic relations with Poland. On March 17, 1938, when the lawlessness in international relations in Europe was nearing a peak, the Polish government, with tacit German consent, delivered to Lithuania an ultimatum, which was backed by the massing of troops on the "demarcation line." [16] Lithuania had no choice but to accept the ultimatum, and relations were restored at least nominally between the two countries. At that time Germany and Poland were on the friendliest terms. Despite Poland's hostile attitude toward Lithuania, the latter kept the most friendly

[15] *The Vilna Question,* p. 91.

[16] See Appendix D for the text of the ultimatum. The "demarcation line" was claimed by the Poles as the legal boundary between Lithuania and Poland but was never recognized by the Lithuanians.

neutrality toward Poland in the hour of distress during the German-Polish war.

On March 22, 1939, Germany, under the threat of invasion, forced Lithuania to surrender Klaipeda. After Poland collapsed in September, 1939, Soviet Russia seized Vilnius and, according to the Mutual Assistance Pact of October 10, 1939,[17] returned it to Lithuania together with 2,569 square miles of territory. On June 15, 1940, Soviet Russia, subsequent to its ultimatum, invaded and occupied Lithuania. Almost exactly a year later, on June 23, 1941, the Lithuanians seized an opportunity to start a violent uprising against the Russians, but already the Germans were pouring in from the south and west. They overran Lithuania, dispersed the newly organized Lithuanian government, and started a new period of oppression, Nazi style.

THE POPULATION PATTERN

The Lithuanians were famous from ancient times for their physical health, strength, and vitality. Even today there is still a substantial percentage of elderly persons who have never taken medicine and have never been seriously ill. In general, Lithuanians are farm-loving people, industrious and peaceful. Being great individualists, the Lithuanians prefer to live on farms because it keeps them close to nature and at the same time affords every man a greater chance of being "his own boss." The cities of Lithuania are therefore inhabited by minorities, mostly Jews. Even in present-day Lithuania, the towns do not show the real character of the nation, as the influx from the farms to the cities has never been strong enough to change the political, economic, and social conditions that have existed for several centuries.

[17] See Appendix E for the text.

According to the census of September 17, 1923, Lithuania had 2,170,616 inhabitants. This number, it was estimated, had increased to 2,575,363 by 1939. However, about 153,-793 were lost by the forced cession to Germany of Klaipeda (Memel) Territory in March, 1939, and about 457,500 were regained through the return of a portion of the Vilnius region in October, 1939. Thus, Lithuania at the end of 1939 had about 2,879,070 inhabitants.[18] But since then still further changes occurred. After the occupation in June, 1940, Soviet Russia started the Sovietization of Lithuania. Those suspected as "enemies of the people" were arrested and deported to the interior of Russia, mostly to Siberia. Conservative estimates put the number of persons so deported at 70,000. In addition, by an agreement concluded between Russian and German governments, about 60,000 persons were "repatriated" by Germany as persons of German extraction. When Germany started the attack on Soviet Russia on June 22, a part of Jewish population fled with the Red Army. Therefore, it is estimated that Lithuania as a consequence of Soviet Russian and German occupation lost about 150,000 inhabitants.

About 76.7 percent of the inhabitants live on farms and villages, while the remaining 23.3 percent live in the towns. The towns are not numerous and in most cases are small. The larger and more important are Vilnius, the capital, with 210,000 inhabitants; Kaunas, with about 130,000 inhabitants; Klaipeda, the Baltic port, with 58,000 inhabitants; Siauliai, an important center of communications and the center of the leather industry, with about 30,000 inhabitants; and Panevezys, an old commercial and administrative center, with 25,000 inhabitants. The average density of the popula-

[18] Centralinis Statistikos Biuras, *Statistikos Biuletenis* (Bulletin of Statistics), Nr. 10., Kaunas, Oct. 1939, p. 1. (Hereafter referred to as S. Biul. 10.)

tion of Lithuania is estimated at 118.6 per square mile. The western and southwestern parts of Lithuania are more densely inhabited, the county of Vilkaviskis having an average population of 147.6 per square mile and the county of Marijampole, 116.8. The southern, northern, and northeastern parts of the country are less densely inhabited than the western. For example, the counties of Seinai, Telsiai, and Zarasai have only 78 inhabitants per square mile.[19]

According to nationality, the inhabitants of Lithuania are divided as in Table 1. The religions are shown in Table 2 and occupations in Table 3.

TABLE 1

NATIONALITIES IN LITHUANIA

NATIONALITY	NUMBER	PERCENT OF TOTAL
Lithuanians	1,739,489	80.60
Jews	154,321	7.15
Germans	88,568	4.10
Poles	65,628	3.04
Russians	50,727	2.34
Latvians	14,930	.69
White Russians	4,421	.21
All others	40,075	1.86

TABLE 2

RELIGIONS

RELIGION	NUMBER	PERCENT
Roman Catholic	1,129,870	80.33
Lutheran (Evangelist)	207,118	9.56
Russian Orthodox	55,122	2.62
All other Christian	1,889	.08
Hebrew	157,527	7.30
All other non-Christian	1,640	.07

[19] C.S.B., *La Lithuanie en chiffres 1918–1928*, Kaunas, 1929, p. 2.

TABLE 3

OCCUPATIONS

OCCUPATION	NUMBER	PERCENT
Agriculture	1,129,870	76.71
Industry and handicraft	94,731	6.43
Transportation and communication	15,585	1.06
Commerce and credit	37,268	2.53
Civil service and professionals	47,408	3.22
Other occupations	148,083	10.05

From the figures in these tables, it can be seen that Lithuania has comparatively small minorities and is predominantly an agricultural country, with more than 76 percent of the population engaged in farming. The percentage of minorities may have been increased somewhat by the changing conditions. The percentage of Jews, no doubt, has risen with the return of Vilnius, which has a large Jewish population. The total percentage of Poles and White Russians will also be somewhat higher than it was when these figures were compiled.

The figures of the German minority, of course, have been completely altered since 1939. After Klaipeda Territory was seized by Germany the percentage of Germans in Lithuania amounted to not more than one and one-half percent of the entire population. With the subsequent repatriation of all Germans from Lithuania in 1941, this minority has wholly disappeared.

Lithuania has no distinctive social classes. Peasants reestablished Lithuania in 1918, and the sons of peasants were running the state affairs until Soviet Russia's occupation on June 15, 1940.

THE LAND AND ITS RESOURCES

Lithuania is situated on the southeastern shore of the Baltic Sea between 53°35′ and 56°27′ north latitude and between 20°57.5′ and east longitude. The two other Baltic states, Latvia and Estonia, are farther north.

The surface of Lithuania is for the most part level, with none of her hills measuring more than 767 feet (234 meters) above sea level. In size, the nation has less than six percent of the territory of Europe, its area being 21,489 square miles. This figure, however, does not include all the territory of ethnographic Lithuania, which is about 33,937 square miles, divided as follows:

	SQ. MI.	SQ. KM.
Lithuania Major	20,389	52,820
Klaipeda (Memel) Territory	1,100	2,850
Lithuania up to March 22, 1939	21,489	55,670
Vilnius Region according to the Peace Treaty of July 12, 1920, with Russia	12,448	32,250
TOTAL	33,937	87,920

According to the Mutual Assistance Treaty between Lithuania and Soviet Russia, concluded October 10, 1939, part of the Vilnius region, about 2,569 square miles (6,656 square kilometers), was returned to Lithuania. However, all figures of economic activity used in this monograph refer to the territory of 21,489 square miles (55,670 square kilometers) that was under the sovereignty of Lithuania from January, 1923, to March 22, 1939.

Lithuania uses a larger percentage of its land for intensive agricultural purposes than its neighboring Baltic states. This may be seen from the comparative figures given in Table 4.

TABLE 4

LAND USE IN THE BALTIC STATES

TYPE OF LAND	LITHUANIA		LATVIA		ESTONIA	
	Thousands of Acres	*Per-cent*	*Thousands of Acres*	*Per-cent*	*Thousands of Acres*	*Per-cent*
Arable land	6,667	48.5	5,243	32.2	2,671	23.9
Meadows and pasture land	2,817	20.5	4,094	25.2	4,305	38.5
Forests	2,599	18.9	4,317	26.6	2,315	20.7
All others	1,673	12.1	2,602	16.0	1,885	16.9
TOTAL	13,756 [a]	100.0	16,256 [b]	100.0	11,176 [c]	100.0

[a] 5,567,000 hectares.
[b] 6,579,000 hectares.
[c] 4,523,000 hectares.

To enable the reader to gain a better understanding and judgment of statistics about the Baltic states given elsewhere in this work, some comparative figures are given in Table 5 regarding the territory and population of Lithuania, Latvia, and Estonia.

Lithuania is lacking in natural resources that are necessary to a well-rounded economic life. One of the country's most serious deficiencies is the absence of its own fuel supply. There is no coal in Lithuania. In 1923 Lithuania imported 5,367,100 litas worth of coal and liquid fuel. By 1928 this figure had almost tripled, imports that year amounting to 14,905,700 litas. The only form of domestic fuel is peat, of which there are 162,221 acres (65,650 hectares). The possibilities of peat have not yet been fully explored, but if peat were made to supplant coal, it is estimated that Lithuania would possess fuel reserves for 132 years.[20]

[20] A. K. Kubilius, *Lietuvos Ukio Perspektyvos* (The Prospects of the National Economy of Lithuania), Kaunas, 1930, p. 190.

TABLE 5

POPULATION DENSITY IN THE BALTIC STATES

	AREA (*Sq. mi.*)	POPULATION	INHABITANTS PER SQ. MI.
Lithuania until March 22, 1939	21,489	2,575,363	117.6
Lithuania after loss of Klaipeda (Memel) Territory	20,389	2,421,570	118.6
Lithuania after the return of Vilnius	22,958	2,879,070	125.4
Latvia (in 1938)	25,395 [a]	1,971,000	78.7 [c]
Estonia (in 1938)	18,354 [b]	1,131,000	61.6 [d]

[a] 65,791 sq. km.
[b] 47,549 sq. km.
[c] 30 per sq. km.
[d] 23.8 per sq. km.

Lithuania has rich deposits of chalk which prove satisfactory for the making of cement, lime, and alabaster, but this industry is still undeveloped. Clay, suited for the ceramic industry, is to be found all over the country, while the eastern shore of the Baltic Sea has been known since ancient times for its amber, "northern gold."

CLIMATE

The climate of Lithuania is of the modified humid continental type. The average temperature is 6.5° Celsius (43.7° Fahrenheit), the warmest month being July, with an average temperature 18.3° Celsius (64.9° F.), and the coldest, January, with an average temperature of 4.8° Celsius below zero (23.4° F.). The ground is frozen for about four months.[21]

[21] C.S.B., S. Biul. 10, 1938, pp. 5–12.

In general, the climate of Lithuania is not so favorable for the cultivating of grain crops as it is for the breeding of livestock. An effort has been made in recent years, under the guidance and encouragement of the country's leading economists, to concentrate on livestock breeding and to reduce grain crop culture. The winters in Lithuania are long, although not cold enough to affect winter crops, which are grown in substantial quantities. Heavy rainfall in the autumn aids in the germination of the winter crops. In 1935, 1,258,085 acres (509,140 hectares), or 18.98 percent of all arable land, were used for the growing of winter rye, while 8,723 acres (3,530 hectares) about 0.12 percent of the arable land, were used for spring rye. Because of the long winters and the concentration on grain culture, a great amount of man power is kept comparatively inactive for several months of the year.

Chapter II

AGRICULTURE

When the Lithuanians, at the end of the first World War, were struggling to reëstablish themselves as an independent country, it was argued by some that Lithuania could not survive as an economic entity. Indicative of the opinion prevailing in the world in those days is a remark of John Foster Bass. Speaking of the relations between Lithuania and Poland and the border dispute, he said:

> It would, therefore, have appeared wise for the Poles to accept the Curzon line as a temporary boundary, until a further settlement could be obtained by agreement with Lithuania and a more settled Russia. This would have these advantages:
>
> First, it would have allayed the Lithuanian hostility to Poland.
>
> *Secondly, it would have afforded Lithuania an opportunity to experience the difficulties, political and economic, which confront small, dependent nations.*[1]

There is no doubt that small nations will continue to have political difficulties so long as international relations are governed by armed force. But even large nations are not impregnable against massive hostile forces and modern military equipment, as was amply proven in 1939 and the subsequent years.

It is a known fact that, refusing to accept the terms of

[1] John Foster Bass, *The Peace Tangle*, New York, 1920, p. 249. The italics are mine.

the Curzon line, the Poles occupied more than one third of Lithuania's territory. But even after this blow Lithuania not only survived as an economic entity, but in twenty-two years of independence made much greater progress economically and culturally than during her 123 years as part of Russia, proving that even a small nation enjoying an independent status can make a tremendously greater advance in her economic and cultural life than the same nation when she is forced to accept "protection."

Even now, while World War II is being waged, voices are heard blaming the small nations which, it is said, aggressors used as tools, playing them against each other only to destroy them later, one by one. While it is true that the small countries were rendered helpless when the mightier ones which had stood on the side of justice were overpowered by the aggressors, nevertheless these small ones cannot be blamed. The fault lies with those big powers which, by disarming themselves, physically and morally encouraged the belligerents.

It is a known fact that the small countries were the most loyal supporters of the League of Nations, though they did not always gain justice, international law not having been enforced as well as it might have been. Nevertheless, the only hope of small nations is the victory of democracy and the rebirth of the League of Nations which will have authority and will not hesitate to exert it, by force if necessary.

There was nothing fundamentally wrong with the League of Nations prior to this second World War, barring the fact that it had no physical power with which to enforce its decisions and consequently hesitated to act on the side of justice in violations of international law. If the League of Nations had not hesitated to act when Vilnius was seized by Poland in 1920, when Japan invaded Manchuria in 1931, and in many other instances in subsequent years, most likely there would have been no breaking of the Versailles Treaty for the purpose of conquest, and, above all, there would be no war today.

GENERAL OUTLINE AND BASIS OF RECONSTRUCTION

As stated before, Lithuania is entirely an agricultural country. During the first twenty-two years of her independence, she focused her attention on the introduction of scientific methods in farming and the development of industries connected with agriculture. She concentrated on the development and production of raw materials in an earnest endeavor to improve her economic status.

The development of world raw-material production from the latter part of the nineteenth century until 1939 may be divided into four periods:

1.—Pre-World War period of normal progress;

2.—The war and post-war period of disturbed development, 1914–22;

3.—Post-war period of progress, beginning with 1923, a seven-year period of progress with moderate fluctuations along lines that followed the same trend as before the war;

4.—Period of disturbed development during the world depression, and of recovery from 1930 until the war of 1939.[2]

1. The pre-war period.—Lithuania then being under the government of Russia, complete economic statistics of that period are not available. On the other hand, the statistical ma-

[2] League of Nations, *Report of the Committee for the Study of the Problem of Raw Materials,* Geneva, 1937, p. 37.

terial collected by the German professor Skalweit [3] refers to a territory somewhat larger than the Lithuania of 1939. His findings, however, give a fairly accurate picture of the state of agriculture in Lithuania before the World War of 1914–18.

The main branches of agriculture in pre-war Lithuania were the cultivation of grain crops, the growing of flax, and the breeding of horses. Dairying, pig breeding, and poultry farming were almost nonexistent.[4]

2. The war and post-war period of disturbed development.—The study of these periods is almost entirely omitted in this volume, as these periods cannot serve for comparison, because almost from the very first days of the war Lithuania was converted into a battlefield for the Russian and German armies. The pursuit of agriculture was impossible throughout most of the period. As late as 1920, when a third of Lithuania was seized by Poland, foreign armies were still trampling the few crops that the farmers were trying to raise. Only after 1920 did Lithuania actually enter upon a comparatively normal economic life.

3 and 4. Post-war periods of progress, depression, and recovery.—Agriculture, the most fundamental economic activity of man, varies from the most primitive cultivation with the hoe to skilled machine-implemented scientific farming. In Lithuania, farming is not mechanized to a great extent, for the use of machinery on small parcels of land is not profitable. Experiments in scientific farming have, however, been undertaken and substantial progress has been made since the World War. Though wheat is mankind's most

[3] B. Skalweit, *Die Landwirtschaft in den litauischen Gouvernements: ihre Grundlagen und Leistungen* (Agriculture in the Lithuanian Gouvernements: Its Foundation and Efficiency), Jena, 1918.

[4] J. Kriksciunas, *Agriculture in Lithuania*, Kaunas, 1938, p. 12.

popular cereal food, rye is the first choice in Lithuania. Only about 8 percent of all the arable land is utilized for wheat, while 19 percent of the land is devoted to the growing of rye. Another of the world's largest crops—corn (maize)—is not grown in Lithuania. The same is true of rice. The more popular grain crops, besides rye, are oats, barley, and wheat. Most favored of root crops in Lithuania are the potato and various species of root vegetables. The sugar beet, entirely unknown before the World War, is now quite popular and is grown in sufficient quantities to supply three sugar refineries. Of the fibers, flax is the only one that is widely grown. Hemp is also produced, but in small quantities and only for the consumption of farmers themselves, who use the fiber for ropes and the seeds for several kinds of food.

Another important branch of the agriculture of Lithuania is livestock breeding, which has been vastly improved and extended since the World War.

Economic reconstruction after the World War was not as general among agricultural countries as it might at first appear. Timoshenko points out several unfavorable factors.[5] First of all, the prices of agricultural commodities began to decline early in the period of prosperity. This affected the purchasing power of agricultural and raw-material producing countries. Another adverse factor was the reëstablishment of a system of agricultural protection in the industrial countries of Europe. Cereal production was given less tariff protection during the earlier post-war period than before the war. In some countries of central Europe, including Germany, tariff protection of grain products was completely discontinued during the first post-war years.

[5] Vladimir P. Timoshenko, *World Agriculture and Depression*, Michigan Business Studies, Vol. V, No. 5, University of Michigan, 1933, pp. 541–663.

Since 1924–25 the policy has been changed and the countries of central Europe have returned to the pre-war methods of tariff protection of their cereal production as well as to the protection of their animal husbandry. This has contributed to duplication in production and to the narrowing of the world market for exported agricultural products, while other factors stimulated the further expansion of agricultural production in the surplus-exporting countries. Exports from agricultural and raw-material producing countries increased very little during the years of prosperity because there was no appreciable increase in the demand for these products in the industrial countries. At the same time, the imports of agricultural countries, consisting mainly of manufactured goods, rose rapidly. The payment balance of agricultural countries could be kept in equilibrium only by an increase in indebtedness or by drawing on the surplus of previous years. For example, in 1924 Lithuania's exports exceeded imports by 60 million litas, while in 1927 imports exceeded exports by 19.8 million litas and in 1938 by 34.2 million litas.[6]

Data on economic activities in Lithuania cover the period up to 1939. With the war of 1939 another period of "disturbed economic development" started; no attempt can be made to analyze this period in this volume, since economic conditions are very unstable and data on economic activities unavailable.

LAND REFORM

One of the factors that contributed most to a complete overhauling of the internal economic and social structure of Lithuania was the land reform, a question which was

[6] Exchange rate: 10 litas to $1.00 until 1933; 6 litas to $1.00, 1935–40.

raised as far back as 1905 by the Lithuanian deputies at the Vilnius diet. That there was a need for reform can be seen from the fact that before the World War, about 450 families possessed 3.5 million acres or 22 percent of all the land. Each of these possessed at least 2,000 acres.[7]

To analyze the political, economic, and social conditions which caused the great part of the land to fall into the hands of a few landlords would require extensive and long study. It may be pointed out, however, that land conveyance was not always effected in an honest way; too often, transfer was forced on peasants by depriving them of owners' rights and making them merely tenants. After the unsuccessful uprisings against the Russian government in 1831 and again in 1863, many participants were sent to Siberia and their lands were confiscated. Some of these lands were later divided into small parcels and distributed among the Russian colonists, while other lands were consolidated into estates (*latifundia*) and, by special decrees of October 4–16, 1835, and December 6, 1842, turned over to families of Russian nobility as *entailed estates*. An estate in this category could not be sold, but, upon the death of the owner, passed on to his eldest son. It was these frozen estates that were the first to be affected by the land reform begun by the Provisional Government of Lithuania in 1918.[8]

It was ordered that all land converted by the Russian decrees of 1835 and 1842 into entailed estates should temporarily be made the state property of Lithuania, to be dis-

[7] Stasys Elsbergas, *Lietuvos Zemes Reforma* (Land Reform of Lithuania), Kaunas, 1935, p. 7.

[8] Salkauskas, K. *Lietuvos Novelos. Veikiančiuju 1935. III. 16 d. Lietuvos istatymu ir isakymu, paskelbtu Vyriausybes Ziniose 1–476 rinkinys* (The Novels of Lithuania. The Laws and Orders of Lithuania, Published in the Government Gazette No. 1–476, Which Are in Force on March 16, 1935), Spaudos Fondas, Kaunas, 1935, p. 324.

posed of eventually by distribution among the landless and the small landowners (those having not more than 12 acres).[9] This decree was legalized by the Preliminary Land Reform Law of August 18, 1920, and its scope was broadened to permit the republic of Lithuania to assume also the ownership of private forests that were larger than 25 *desimtines* (one *desimtine* is equal to about 2.7 acres).[10] This law was a tentative one in that it contained no provision for the distribution of the expropriated property.

The Land Reform Law in its final draft, consisting of twelve sections and subdivided into seventy-seven paragraphs, was ratified in 1922.[11] The first section outlines the composition of the lands reserved for distribution, defining particularly the land to be taken into the distribution reserve. This action also enabled the state to take over the private property of those who had served in the post-war German armed bands of Bermont and Virgolicz and of those who had worked or were still working against the independence of Lithuania. Estates exceeding 200 acres and owned by one person or one family were also to be taken for land reform purposes.[12] Later the limit was raised to 321 acres (150 hectares). The second section of the Land Reform Law provides that the biggest and least active estates shall be among the first to be appropriated for land reform purposes. The third section defines the types of prospective recipients of the reapportioned land parcels. It states mainly that heads of families of landless peasants, farm laborers, and small landowners are entitled to share in the land distribution. Those farmers, or their lawful successors, from whom land was

[9] Elsbergas, *op. cit.*, p. 7.

[10] *Vyriausybes Zinios,* Nr. 45 eil. 454 (Government Gazette No. 45, Part 454). Hereafter referred to as V.Z.

[11] *Ibid.,* Nr. 83 eil. 721.

[12] *Ibid.,* Nr. 324 eil. 2218.

seized by the government in 1861 and 1863 are to receive priority over all others. Each head of a family may receive not more than 49.4 acres (20 hectares). Land is also to be distributed to public schools, schools of agriculture, and other institutions of learning and culture as well as to hospitals, sanatoriums, asylums, and other social and public organizations.

The land is divided into four classes, graded according to the fertility of the soil. The new owners have to pay equal annual installments for their land for thirty-six years. The rate to be paid varies from 180 to 252 litas per hectare (2.471 acres) for first-class land, depending on its location; 90 to 126 litas for second-class; 36 to 54 litas for third-class, and 18 to 27 litas for fourth-class. No interest accumulates on the unpaid balance except on due shares which are not paid in the time prescribed.[13]

The only recipients of land exempted from all payments are volunteer soldiers in the Lithuanian war for independence and their families.

Former owners of the lands taken for land reform purposes were entitled to compensation. Payment was to be made with government bonds bearing three percent interest and redeemable at any time not later than thirty-six years from the date of issue. Paragraph 58 of the Land Reform Law prescribes that the compensation for the land shall be a fair price based on valuations existing in the period between 1910 and 1914. As the Land Reform Law was passed on April 3, 1922, when *Obost* marks[14] were in circulation, the compensation was to be paid in this currency. (One Russian ruble was made equal to two *Obost* marks.) Paragraph 59 provides that the highest amount paid may not exceed

[13] Salkauskas, *op. cit.*, pp. 325–32.

[14] See, p. 102 below, section on Finance.

480 marks per hectare. Because the mark fell in value, the reward was comparatively small when translated into litas. It is estimated that the total amount paid by the government for expropriated land up to 1935 was 40 million litas.

In accordance with this law, the land transfer up to the end of 1939 involved 1,774,099 acres (717,968 hectares), of which a substantial part was handed over for cultural and other public uses, being given for schools, cemeteries, municipalities, public playgrounds, and so on.

TABLE 6

THE LAND INVOLVED FOR REDISTRIBUTION BETWEEN 1919 AND 1939

	ACRES
I. Land distributed for permanent ownership	
1. To private schools, organizations, asylums, etc.	2,291
2. To parish churches	3,981
3. For cemeteries	1,003
4. To employees and laborers for homes	8,110
5. To new settlers	893,392
6. Added to small farms	222,951
TOTAL	1,131,728
II. Land distributed for temporary use	
1. To public schools and other governmental institutions	86,070
2. To municipalities and their institutions (hospitals, asylums, public parks, etc.)	6,158
3. To private persons and organizations	26,539
4. For community pastures	72,170
TOTAL	190,937
III. For miscellaneous uses	451,434
GRAND TOTAL OF LAND AFFECTED BY THE LAND REFORM ACT	1,774,099

According to the agricultural census of 1930, the number of farms in Lithuania and their areas are as stated in Table 7.

TABLE 7

CENSUS OF FARMS

FARM SIZE (*Acres*)	NUMBER OF FARMS	COMBINED AREA (*Acres*)
2.5– 12.5	53,463	380,722
12.5– 25.0	78,237	1,440,338
25.0– 37.5	59,572	1,788,349
37.5– 50.0	33,236	1,408,275
50.0– 75.0	34,197	2,042,511
75.0–125.0	20,597	1,885,111
125.0–250.0 and over	8,078	1,725,742
TOTAL	287,380	10,671,048

Through the land reform, over 45,000 new farms have been established and over 200,000 persons (including new settlers and their families) have been provided with regular occupation and permanent homes. This undoubtedly has brought beneficial results to the social and economic life of the country.[15] Moreover, the land reform has undoubtedly been a means of substantially raising the country's productivity, to the benefit of both the state and the individual farmer.

When Soviet Russia occupied Lithuania on June 15, 1940, a still more radical "land reform" was proclaimed by the Soviet-appointed puppet government. All land was proclaimed state property. Consequently, the farmer-owners suddenly became only managers of government property and, therefore, could not sell, exchange, or give away their

[15] Kriksciunas, *op. cit.*, p. 34; Elbergas, *op. cit.*, pp. 64–68.

land. Seventy-four acres (30 hectares) was the maximum allowed each family to manage.

Several thousand formerly landless farmers who obtained a few acres through this Soviet "land reform" and whose popular support the Soviet government was seeking found themselves unable to till the allotted land because they had no tools, seed, or livestock and could not secure any aid from the government. The Soviet policy was to force them all into so-called "collective farms" (kolkhoz).

The majority of the farms of 80 hectares (198 acres) or over were not distributed at all but converted into government farms (sovkhoz) controlled through commissars.

Those who were allowed to keep 30 hectares (74 acres) were called "kulaks," and such high taxes were imposed upon them that they were forced to join the government-fostered collective farms.

As indicated by Table 7, before the Soviet Russian occupation there were 287,380 separate farms in Lithuania, ranging in area from 2.5 to 250 acres. These farms, on the basis of productive capacity, were classified into three groups.

The first group was comprised of the self-sufficient farms, ranging in acreage from 2.50 to 30 acres. Farmers in this group raised sufficient grain to maintain their families and kept one or two horses for work, one to four milk cows, and some poultry; thus they themselves produced most of their food. They had little to sell and bought little from the town. At the end of 1939, about 160,000 farms or 56 percent of all farms of Lithuania were in this group.

The second group was comprised of farms of between 30 and 70 acres which produced substantial quantities of agricultural products for the market. Although the farming system of this group was similar to that of the first one to the extent that these farmers produced various kinds of agricultural products, they usually concentrated more specially on one branch of farming, such as dairying or grain raising. About 100,000 farms belonged to this group.

Farms exceeding 70 acres belonged to the third group and stood highest in independent Lithuania from the point of view of the quality and quantity of their products. There were about 27,000 farms in this group. It was mainly this and the second group which supplied the bulk of agricultural products for export. It was also this third group and to a degree the second which first felt the ruin of Sovietization. Most of the farms in the third group were reduced to not more than 74 acres so that the farming inventory and buildings were not suitable to the smaller parcels of land. A substantial part of them was converted into government farms (*sovkhoz*). At the same time pressure was put on the second group by imposing exorbitant taxes in order to make it disintegrate as rapidly as possible.

Taking into consideration the area of land utilized by each group, it might be deduced that in normal times the first group produced 20 percent of the entire amount sold on the market, while the second and third groups produced the remaining 80 percent, or 40 percent each. From this it would appear that the capacity of agricultural production in Lithuania during the Soviet Russian occupation dropped at least 40 percent.

When the Germans occupied Lithuania in June, 1941, they found the Bolshevik-introduced system convenient to some extent for the expropriation of the country economically. They restored the system of private ownership, but had not returned, up to the end of 1941, farms to the original owners. Even those farmers who were left managers of their small farms (not exceeding 74 acres) during the Sovietization were not reëstablished as owners but were continued as managers, so that the German masters might conveniently remove them from the farms at any moment.

Latest unofficial reports indicate that several hundred German managers have been sent to Lithuania to manage the former government farms. Apparently Germans are keeping the bigger farms for colonization in the event they win this second world war. No doubt, it will take several years after this war to regain the degree of agricultural production achieved during the peace period after 1918.

COÖPERATIVES

Coöperatives are the backbone of progress and of economic reconstruction in Lithuania. Although the first coöperative societies in Lithuania originated as far back as the end of the eighteenth century, the wider coöperative movement was begun only in 1881, when the first consumer coöperative societies were organized by I. Ivanavicius. Ivanavicius acknowledges that his inspiration for coöperative work was obtained through traveling in Western Europe —Denmark, Germany, and Switzerland. He was the initiator and a member of the first coöperative dairy society, Birute, which was organized in 1889 and of which large and influential landowners of the district of Raseiniai were members. In 1912 there were in Lithuania 52 consumer coöperative societies with 8,193 members. For better coördination in this work, these individual coöperative societies attempted to establish a central organization, but they were refused permission by the Russian government.[16]

[16] Petras Salcius, *Kooperacija; Kooperacijos paskaitu kursas* (Coöperation; Lectures on Coöperation), Kaunas, 1931, p. 195.

Vartotoju Bendroviu Sajunga Kooperatorius (The Union of Consumers' Coöperative Societies) was finally organized in 1915, but because of the war it was unable to start its work.

The second group of importance before the World War consisted of the credit coöperative societies. They were started in 1871, and in 1889 there were 31 of them in the provinces (gouvernements) of Kaunas, Vilnius, and Suvalkai. By 1915 their number reached 155.

The third group of coöperatives before the World War in Lithuania was made up of the agricultural coöperative societies. Their purpose was to raise the standard of agriculture and to introduce and demonstrate to the farmers modern scientific farming methods. These coöperative societies endeavored to supply farmers with fertilizers and farming machinery. The most successful one in that field was Zagre, which was established in 1907 and had by 1913 twenty branches. There were also numerous small coöperative farm groups.

During the first World War most of the coöperatives collapsed. Yet it was these early organizations that prepared the ground for a country-wide spread of coöperatives after the war.

That coöperative activity was strongly encouraged by the government may be observed from the Union Law of the Coöperative Societies, passed on February 7, 1919, which states:

> Our country is a country of farms and there is no big capital concentrated in one place; nevertheless, there is much money in the same place, which may be concentrated and made useful through coöperatives. . . . The Ministry of Commerce and Industry is of the opinion that coöperatives will give the country a useful or-

ganization for the distribution of goods in markets and will abolish speculation among certain merchants who raise the prices spuriously by storing goods and not releasing them to the markets.[17]

It must be remembered that this opinion was expressed shortly after the war, when the great shortage of goods was felt everywhere.

In addition, a special Department of Coöperation was created as part of the Ministry of Commerce and Industry. Although the government encouraged coöperation, it did not interfere with sound private initiative, particularly in later years, when the post-war conditions were more settled. In 1920 the Department of Coöperation was abolished because coöperation in Lithuania became so strong that it no longer required any special attention from the government.

Before Soviet occupation in 1940 most of the coöperative establishments enjoyed tax exemption privileges. According to the Commerce, Industry, Credit, and Trade Profit Taxation Law,[18] the following coöperative establishments were to be free from profit taxes:

1. Consumers' coöperative societies whose capital did not exceed 50,000 litas.
2. All credit and agricultural coöperative societies.
3. All kinds of coöperative unions.
4. All those coöperative societies which did business exclusively among their members, even though their capital was in excess of 50,000 litas.

Undoubtedly those exceptions placed coöperative establishments in a somewhat privileged position in the competitive field as compared with private enterprises.

[17] Salcius, *op. cit.*, p. 203.
[18] V.Z., Nr. 168.

Table 8 shows the number and types of coöperative societies in the years 1937 to 1939.[19]

TABLE 8

COÖPERATIVE SOCIETIES OF LITHUANIA
1937–39

TYPE OF COÖPERATIVE	NUMBER OF SOCIETIES REGISTERED		
	1937	*1938*	*1939*
1. Credit	408	398	401
2. Stores and consumers' coöperatives	248	251	275
3. Manufacturing	226	228	224
4. Insurance	1	2	2
5. Nonclassified	375	409	430
TOTAL	1,258	1,288	1,332

1. Credit coöperatives.—Credit coöperative societies were the first to be reëstablished, after the war, in towns and townships. Most of them were organized by the Jewish population and served small merchantmen. Among the farmers, they were organized only after the introduction of stabilized currency, the litas. In 1923, 129 credit coöperative societies were organized; in 1924, 107; in 1925, 136. There are in Lithuania three kinds in this category: town coöperatives (mostly Jewish People's Banks), farmer credit coöperatives, and farmer saving and loan associations. The Jewish People's Banks Union (Zydu Liaudies Banku Sajunga) does no active business, but acts rather as an ideological center and coördinator. This union had 101 member banks in 1930. In recent years the number of credit coöperatives diminished somewhat, as may be seen from Table 8. This is partly due

[19] C.S.B., 1939, pp. 263–65.

to the merging of two or three small units into one. Evidence of this is the fact that membership in these societies increased instead of decreasing. In 1935, there were 119,687 members, of whom 77,553 were farmers; in 1936, 121,169 members, of whom 79,392 were farmers; in 1938, 117,155 members and in 1939, 119,326 members.

The financial position of all the credit coöperative societies in 1939 is indicated by the following statistics: total capital, 14,473,200 litas, of which membership shares accounted for 7,903,200 litas; reserve capital, 3,311,700 litas; and other capital, 1,591,100 litas. Total deposits in credit coöperative societies in 1939 amounted to 29,857,700 litas; borrowings from the banks, 22,554,500 litas; credits to members and the rest, 60,823,900 litas.

The farmer credit coöperatives are assembled in the Coöperation Bank of Lithuania (Lietuvos Kooperacijos Bankas).

2. *Stores and consumers' coöperatives.*—In 1939 there were 275 coöperative stores and consumers' coöperative societies, as well as one union, the Central Union of Agricultural Coöperative Societies of Lithuania, known under the trade name of Lietukis. The coöperative stores, as well as consumers' coöperatives, trade in colonial goods, while the Union, with its branches, buys farm products for export (mostly grain crops, linseed, and flax), and sells agricultural machinery, petroleum products, salt, cement, fertilizers, and so on.

The Central Union of Agricultural Coöperative Societies, Lietukis, was established in 1923; financially, it is one of the strongest coöperative unions of Lithuania; and it is the most popular. The Union is the largest exporter of grain in Lithuania: before the 1940 occupation it handled almost the entire grain export.[20]

Lietukis, which comprised 145 coöperative societies in its membership in 1939, maintained 16 branch establishments in Lithuania, in addition to its central establishment in Kaunas. It operated in 1939 three grain elevators, one of 3,000 metric tons' capacity in Klaipeda (Memel), another of 3,250 metric tons' capacity in Siauliai, and a third of 2,250 tons' capacity in Kaunas. Furthermore, it possessed a central flax warehouse at Siauliai and 18 grain warehouses at various other places.[21]

Lietukis handles the largest percentage in the total turnover of many commodities of Lithuania: import of fertilizers, 100 percent; salt import, 92.9; import of agricultural machinery, 80; cement import, 42; import of petroleum products, 40; import of herring, 10; iron import, 5; export of grain, 85; export of flax, 27; sale of sugar, 89.[22]

The growth and expansion of business of coöperative stores, Lietukis, and other coöperative societies in the last eleven years before the second world war is indicated by Table 9.[23]

Furthermore, it is worthy of mention that in 1926 Lietukis acquired 45 percent of the capital stock of the Maistas Corporation, whose principal business is the keeping of stockyards in which livestock is prepared for export. With the acquisition of this stock interest Lietukis indirectly entered the export trade in meat and live animals. Lietukis was also

20 Kriksciunas, *op. cit.*, p. 141.

21 *Lietukis, Lietuvos Zemes Ukio Kooperatyvu Sajunga* (Lietukis, the Central Union of Agricultural Coöperative Societies), Kaunas, 1934.

22 *Report of the Chamber of Commerce, Industry and Crafts*, Kaunas, 1938, p. 113. Referred to hereafter as *Report*.

23 *Ibid.*, p. 112.

TABLE 9

SALES OF THE COÖPERATIVE SOCIETIES

(In Thousands of Litas)

YEAR	LIETUKIS	TRADE COÖPERATIVES	PIENOCENTRAS[a]	TOTAL
1928	12,129	23,520	13,662	49,311
1929	29,393	52,255	25,999	108,647
1930	23,117	44,992	43,854	111,963
1931	36,743	44,950	46,102	127,795
1932	28,853	37,314	45,182	111,349
1933	32,063	37,534	36,163	105,760
1934	32,617	37,342	36,329	111,288
1935	60,530	46,427	42,438	149,395
1936	73,715	55,560	55,897	185,172
1937	72,360	65,046	65,730	205,599
1938	113,909	95,165	76,920	283,884
1939	138,911	114,285	67,745	320,941

[a] Reference on Pienocentras is given in Section 3 below, on production coöperative societies.

the initiator of coöperative dairies and creameries, which later developed into a separate Central Union of Dairy Coöperative Societies of Lithuania, the Pienocentras.

After Soviet Russian occupation Lietukis was made a government agency with all its branches and continued to function until the German invasion. The Germans in turn took control of Lietukis with all its property, and the German Economic Command (Wirtschaftskommando) issued an order on August 23, 1941, to all the branches of Lietukis, as well as to the agricultural and consumers' coöperative societies, to submit reports on fabrics and other merchandise in its possession and at the same time forbade selling any of the merchandise. It would appear that all the merchandise was confiscated by the Germans.

On September 7 the Kaunas radio broadcast an order by German Commissar for Lithuania von Renteln whereby the purchase of grain was permitted exclusively to Lietukis. From this order alone it is obvious that Lietukis has been turned into agency serving German war purposes.

Deserving of mention in this group is Spaudos Fondas, a coöperative publishing concern with branch stores in every larger town throughout Lithuania for promoting the sale of books and stationery. After Soviet Russian occupation it met the same fate as Lietukis. On August 5, 1940, a decision of the Government Nationalization Committee (Valstybine Nacionalizavimo Komisija), dated August 3, was published, announcing that Spaudos Fondas with all its branches was nationalized.[24]

3. Production coöperatives.—A very important and comparatively young branch of agricultural life in Lithuania, the dairy coöperative societies, forms a part of this third group. As mentioned before, prior to 1926 dairying activities were a department of Lietukis. With the rapid growth of coöperative creameries, it was decided in October, 1926, to withdraw from Lietukis and to organize the Central Union of Dairy Coöperative Societies of Lithuania (Centraline Lietuvos Pieno Perdirbimo Bendroviu Sajunga), known briefly as Pienocentras. The task of Pienocentras is to encourage milk production, develop and improve manufacture, and establish a good rating for Lithuanian milk products in the world market; and to organize coöperative dairies and creameries, coördinate their work, and diminish administration expenses through strong central organization.

In 1938 Pienocentras had a membership of 185 dairy co-

[24] *Tiesa,* No. 44, Aug. 5, 1940. (*Tiesa* [Truth] was the daily of the Lithuanian Communist Party during Soviet occupation.)

operative societies with 2,105 milk-skimming stations. Pienocentras also exports eggs, in which branch it has attained an almost complete monopoly. For example, in 1939 it handled over 96 percent of the total egg export. The growth and development of Pienocentras may be seen from Table 10,[25] which shows that the work of Pienocentras is a real

TABLE 10

TOTAL TURNOVER OF PIENOCENTRAS

(In Thousands of Litas)

YEAR	TOTAL TURNOVER	TOTAL OF EXPORTS	EXPORTS OF BUTTER	EXPORTS OF EGGS	PIENOCENTRAS'S SHARE IN EXPORTS OF LITHUANIA (*Percent*)
1927	5,981	3,971	3,950	—	1.6
1928	13,662	10,437	10,437	—	4.1
1929	25,999	20,888	20,786	102	6.3
1930	43,854	35,200	34,866	334	10.5
1931	46,102	37,790	37,055	735	13.8
1932	45,182	37,079	36,045	1,034	19.6
1933	36,163	29,909	29,150	789	18.7
1934	36,329	30,231	28,816	1,397	20.5
1935	42,438	35,948	33,866	2,046	23.6
1936	55,897	48,228	42,042	6,151	25.3
1937	65,730	54,470	47,065	5,923	26.1
1938	76,920	65,300	55,131	7,833	24.2
1939	67,745	52,100	43,739	8,196	25.7

success not only in attaining a milk-and-egg monopoly in Lithuania but also in encouraging and developing this branch of agriculture. At the end of 1939 all the dairy coöperative societies of Lithuania had 21,701 members as against 18,372 in 1938 and 14,817 in 1937. In 1939 they had 106,605 regular

[25] C.S.B., volumes for 1927 to 1939.

milk suppliers as against 101,348 in 1938 and 69,741 in 1934.

Pienocentras with all its departments continued to function throughout the Soviet Russian occupation, although it was transformed into a government agency. In June, 1941, when the Soviet Russian occupation was replaced by the German occupation, Pienocentras came under the control of the German Economic Command (Wirtschaftskommando), also as government agency. In September, 1941, German Commissar for Lithuania von Renteln issued an order granting monopoly to Pienocentras in the business of dairy products and at the same time forbidding anybody to trade in milk products. Since Pienocentras has a wide organization throughout Lithuania, it is very convenient for the Germans in their control of milk production and in their efforts to extract from Lithuania a maximum of milk products. Of course no statistical data is available for Pienocentras's economic activities during the periods of German and Russian occupation.

Deserving of mention in this group is a local grocery trade coöperative society in Kaunas called Parama which owns and operates thirty modern grocery stores, as well as the largest and most modern bakery in Lithuania, with an annual production valued at about six million litas. Its fate under the German occupation is similar to that of Pienocentras.

4 and 5. Insurance and nonclassified coöperatives.—These two groups are of minor importance in the economic life of Lithuania. Insurance, still undeveloped there, is one of the fields open for coöperation in the future. In 1938 there were two insurance coöperative societies with 7,486 members. Insurance premiums collected in 1938 amounted to 355,495 litas, which, compared with the development of other cooperative branches, is a small sum. In the unclassified group in the year 1939 there were 430 societies with a membership of 4,581. The total membership of all coöperative societies in 1939 was 161,256.

All the coöperative unions and bigger coöperative societies have representatives in the Council of Coöperatives of Lithuania (Lietuvos Kooperatyvu Taryba), which was formally chartered on January 30, 1925. The task of the Council is to encourage coöperative movement, to maintain close ties among coöperatives in Lithuania and in foreign countries, and to represent them in the government institutions and public organizations. The Council publishes the magazines *Talka* (Coöperation) and *Bendras Darbas* (Coöperative Work).[26]

In short, it may be said that coöperation has played an important role in the economic reconstruction and development of Lithuania since 1918. Coöperative institutions have increased the purchasing power of the farmers, both as producers and as consumers. At the same time they have furthered economic progress both by increasing productivity and by improving the quality of many products.

GRAIN CULTURE

Grain culture, which has been known in Lithuania since ancient times, was the backbone of the country's agriculture before the World War of 1914–18. Though there has been a tendency since 1926 to concentrate more on livestock breeding and dairying, grain culture still is the dominating feature of Lithuania's agriculture.

In recent years there has been a yearly production of about 1.6 to 1.7 million metric tons of grain, with only a

[26] Salcius, *op. cit.*, pp. 230–31.

small part of this available for export. Almost half of all the arable land of Lithuania is used for grain culture, a fact that is evident from Table 12. Although the amount of arable land used for grain culture increases slowly, the exports of grain have varied widely. The heavy grain exports in 1935

TABLE 11

EXPORTS OF GRAIN 1924–39 [a]

YEAR	GRAIN EXPORTED [b] (*Metric tons*)	VALUE (*1,000 litas*)
1924	24,966	10,022
1926	16,541	9,894
1928	12,310	6,377
1930	40,664	11,526
1932	7,035	2,268
1934	25,504	4,682
1935	162,023	20,465
1936	130,562	14,578
1937	5,795	1,628 [c]
1938	132,379	21,696
1939	85,365	11,700

[a] In the statistics of grain exports are included not only rye, wheat, oats, and barley but also the seeds of vetch, peas, buckwheat, chick-peas, and lentils.

[b] The metric ton or 10 quintals = 36.743 U.S. bushels of wheat or potatoes, 39.369 U.S. bushels of rye or linseed, 45.931 U.S. bushels of barley, 68.894 U.S. bushels of oats, according to the League of Nations' *Statistical Year Book of 1940*.

[c] Kriksciunas, *op. cit.*, p. 104, for the period 1924–37.

and 1936, which according to Professor Kriksciunas [27] may be regarded as accidental, were made possible by an exceptionally large yield in 1934 and 1935. The bulk of production is intended for home consumption.

The most popular grain crops in Lithuania are winter

[27] Kriksciunas, *op. cit.*, p. 105.

rye, winter wheat, oats, and barley; the respective importance of each is indicated by the proportion of the land used for various crops, as shown in Table 12.

TABLE 12

LAND USED FOR VARIOUS CROPS

CROPS	1909–13 [a] (1,000 acres)	1938 [b] (1,000 acres)	PERCENTAGE OF ALL ARABLE LAND
Rye (winter and spring)	1,365.0	1,304.8	19.2
Wheat (winter and spring)	202.0	500.5	7.4
Oats	783.8	877.4	13.0
Barley	452.7	536.3	8.1
Buckwheat	16.1	19.6	.3
TOTAL GRAIN	2,819.6 [c]	3,238.6 [d]	48.0
Legumes	140.8	192.7	2.8
Potatoes	294.3	459.7	6.8
Sugar beets, fodder beets, carrots, and turnips	([e])	160.0	2.4
Clover and other grass fodder	([e])	1,378.2	20.3
Flax	([e])	192.5	2.8
Vegetables	136.4	63.1	.9

[a] J. Kriksciunas, *Die litauische Landwirtschaft* (Lithuanian Agriculture), Kaunas, 1933, p. 133.

[b] C.S.B., 1938, pp. 114–17.

[c] 1,141,100 hectares.

[d] 1,310,640 hectares.

[e] Figures not available.

In general, there is a tendency to reduce rye cultivation. For instance, the total of 1,365,000 acres used for rye in the years 1909–13 is 7.2 percent greater than was used in the same territory in the post-World War period.

In Lithuania rye is used principally for a special dark

bread and various kinds of gruels. That Lithuania is the greatest rye producer of the three Baltic states, Estonia, Latvia, and Lithuania, is shown by Table 13.

TABLE 13

PRODUCTION OF RYE IN THE BALTIC STATES[a]

(*In Thousands of Quintals*[b])

YEAR	LITHUANIA	LATVIA	ESTONIA
1925–29 (av.)	5,175	2,371	1,508
1930–34 (av.)	5,746	3,148	2,013
1935	6,406	3,639	1,728
1936	5,413	2,860	4,215
1937	6,069	4,215	2,115
1938	6,237	3,802	1,880
1939	6,510	4,291	2,280

[a] League of Nations, *Statistical Year-Book of the League of Nations,* 1937–38; C.S.B., 1938, p. 114.

[b] One quintal equals 220.46 pounds. See footnote b of Table 11 for equivalent in U.S. bushels.

Wheat is also one of the important food products of Lithuania. In the pre-war period of 1909–13, 202,000 acres were used annually for wheat, while in 1935, 535,009 acres were used for this crop, of which 414,041 acres, or 77.2 percent, were used for winter wheat and 301,383 acres, or 22.8 percent, for spring wheat.[28] The growing of wheat in Lithuania is increasing much faster than the growing of any other grain. In 1938 about two and a half times more land was used for wheat than in 1909–13. This increase may be observed particularly regarding spring wheat.

From the data of Table 14 we see that Lithuania produces more wheat than either of the other two Baltic states. Since bread in Lithuania is made principally of rye flour, there is

[28] *Lietuvos Surasymas,* 1935, p. 18.

TABLE 14

PRODUCTION OF WHEAT IN THE BALTIC STATES

(In Thousands of Quintals)

YEAR	LITHUANIA	LATVIA	ESTONIA
1925–29 (av.)	1,653	626	275
1930–34 (av.)	2,475	1,498	600
1935	2,747	1,775	617
1936	2,197	1,435	662
1937	2,207	1,715	758
1938	2,512	1,918	861
1939	2,565	1,974	855

a considerable surplus of wheat; the greater part of this surplus is exported and the rest is used for the feeding of home fowl and livestock. As the climate of Lithuania is favorable for wheat growing, further expansion in the size of the wheat crop may be expected.

Oats, which are used mostly for livestock fodder, especially for horses, have almost no use in Lithuania as a food for the population. This crop had expanded substantially in the post-World War period. In 1909–13 it was included with fodder mixture, this entire category accounting for 783,801 acres, while in 1938, 877,400 acres were used for oats alone and another 277,246 acres were used for the growing of fodder mixture.

Barley is used in Lithuania chiefly as fodder for pigs. As pig breeding has expanded since the World War, a larger area is being used for barley growing. It is estimated that in the period 1909–13, 452,700 acres were used for that crop; in 1935 the figure increased to 507,963 acres, in 1938 to 536,300 acres, and further expansion was expected under normal conditions.

TABLE 15

PRODUCTION OF OATS IN THE BALTIC STATES

(In Thousands of Quintals) [a]

YEAR	LITHUANIA	LATVIA	ESTONIA
1925–29 (av.)	3,105	2,485	1,211
1930–34 (av.)	3,788	3,453	1,456
1935	3,995	3,859	1,344
1936	3,320	2,844	1,138
1937	3,878	4,050	1,391
1938	4,200	4,454	1,773
1939	4,106	4,498	1,498

[a] Conversion coefficients: see footnote b of Table 11.

TABLE 16

PRODUCTION OF BARLEY IN THE BALTIC STATES

(In Thousands of Quintals) [a]

YEAR	LITHUANIA	LATVIA	ESTONIA
1925–29 (av.)	2,199	1,551	1,113
1930–34 (av.)	2,336	1,969	1,107
1935	2,516	2,046	918
1936	2,330	1,650	868
1937	2,740	2,184	809
1938	2,713	2,107	968
1939	2,571	2,088	899

[a] See footnote b of Table 11 for conversion coefficients.

ROOT CROPS

Before the World War, root crops were not as important as they have since become in independent Lithuania. Although potatoes were grown and used widely before the war of 1914–18, the area given over to potato growing has expanded more than 45 percent since the pre-war years. The bulk of the potato crop is used as fodder for pigs, a smaller quantity is consumed as food by the people, and the rest goes for distilling purposes.

Beets were grown in pre-war Lithuania, but in small quantities and mainly for human food. With the development of livestock breeding, beet growing for fodder has substantially expanded.

The sugar beet, unknown in Lithuania in the pre-war period, has shown a spectacular rise; 20,000 acres of sugar beets supply the country's three sugar refineries. The following is the record of sugar-beet cultivation in recent years: 1931—6,970 acres; 1932—13,146 acres; 1933—9,887 acres; 1934—9,637 acres; 1935—17,297 acres; [29] 1937—20,336 acres; 1938—21,002 acres; 1939—22,250 acres.[30]

TABLE 17

PRODUCTION OF VARIOUS ROOT CROPS IN THE BALTIC STATES

(In Thousands of Quintals) [a]

YEAR	LITHUANIA	LATVIA	ESTONIA
POTATOES			
1925–29 (av.)	14,645	7,750	7,143
1930–34 (av.)	19,870	12,649	8,683
1935	17,738	14,612	8,927
1936	21,112	16,115	10,306
1937	25,099	17,820	9,856
1938	21,182	17,553	9,976
1939	23,548	16,559	8,740

[29] *Lietuvos Surasymas*, 1935, p. 24.
[30] C.S.B., 1939.

YEAR	LITHUANIA	LATVIA	ESTONIA
SUGAR BEETS			
1928–29	—	20	—
1929–30	—	35	—
1930–31	—	69	—
1931–32	67	94	—
1932–33	164	245	—
1933–34	73	291	—
1934–35	137	539	—
1935–36	198	451	—
1936–37	245	382	—
1937–38	257	442	—
1938–39 [b]	208	296	—

[a] Conversion coefficients: see footnote b of Table 11.
[b] *Revue internationale d'agriculture,* 1940, No. 2.

FLAX

Lithuania is one of the chief flax-producing countries in Europe, for the climate and the soil are very favorable for the cultivation of this crop. It is to be noted that in spite of its small area Lithuania ranks as the third flax exporter of the world, being surpassed only by Soviet Russia and Poland. About 200,000 acres, or a little more than three percent of all the arable land in Lithuania, is used for flax growing. Although this is a comparatively small percentage, the income derived therefrom is high. The income from flax and linseed exports in 1920–36 was greater than that from butter, pigs and pork, eggs, or grain.[31]

Because there are no uniform standards for the preparation of the flax, the export products vary in quality. For example, in southern Lithuania flax is plucked out only after full maturity. Later it is submitted to a process of dew retting

[31] Kriksciunas, *op. cit.*, p. 103. See Table 19 for figures.

instead of being water retted as in other parts of Lithuania. Prepared by such methods, flax fiber is of low quality, although this is offset by a rich yield of valuable linseed. In other parts of Lithuania flax is plucked before reaching full maturity. Flax plucked at this state produces linseed of low quality, but the flax fiber is undoubtedly very strong and fine.[32]

The concentration of flax exports since 1932 in the coöperative concern Lietukis has raised the quality and reputation of Lithuanian flax. Continued progress in this respect will no doubt be reflected in better prices and greater profits.

TABLE 18

PRODUCTION OF FLAX IN THE BALTIC STATES AND POLAND

(In Thousands of Quintals)

YEAR	LITHUANIA	LATVIA	ESTONIA	POLAND
1925–29 (av.)	364	221	100	561
1930–34 (av.)	208	141	66	323
1934	222	162	71	308
1935	319	248	105	398
1936	288	185	87	372
1937	313	231	103	381
1938	258	214	74	399
1939	289	192	62	(*a*)

[a] Figure not available.

The importance of flax, tow, and linseed in the exports of Lithuania may be observed from the fact that in 1924 they constituted 26 percent of Lithuania's total exports; in 1926, 7 percent; in 1928, 20 percent; in 1930, 10 percent; in 1937, 15 percent; in 1938, 11 percent; and in 1939, 17 percent.

[32] Kriksciunas, *op. cit.*, p. 101.

TABLE 19

EXPORTS OF LITHUANIA'S FLAX PRODUCTS

YEAR	FLAX AND TOW: QUANTITY EXPORTED (1,000 metric tons)	FLAX AND TOW: VALUE (Millions of litas)	LINSEED: QUANTITY EXPORTED (1,000 metric tons)	LINSEED: VALUE (Millions of litas)
1924	14.0	52.75	18.6	16.29
1926	19.7	56.93	25.8	18.04
1928	13.2	46.59	77.0	6.18
1930	10.2	19.59	20.1	14.21
1932	9.0	9.12	7.7	2.46
1934	10.2	11.19	6.4	2.01
1936	19.7	25.12	23.8	6.80
1937	16.1	24.00	20.7	7.10
1938	18.8	24.82	5.6	1.98
1939	20.0	30.31	10.3	4.16

DAIRY PRODUCTS

Butter and cheese were produced in pre-war Lithuania, but these items became available in increasing quantities for export only after the World War. In 1909–14, only some of the bigger landlords (farmers owning 200 acres or more) had their own creameries, but most of the middle-class and small farmers prepared milk products mainly for their own consumption, sending only a small portion to near-by township markets. In 1901, forty-eight landlords organized the creamery Birute whose yearly exports of butter reached 620,000 pounds. But the World War which disorganized the national economy of Lithuania also ruined the dairy co-operatives. Not only were the dairies destroyed but the country was deprived of its sources of supply, for almost half of the cattle were slaughtered for meat by various armies.[33]

Shortly after the World War there was great demand for milk products in Germany and prices were high. It was possible to sell milk and milk products even of low quality, especially in the border districts of Germany. In 1924–25 the conditions began to change. Germany returned to the pre-war methods of tariff protection and adopted the policy of economic self-sufficiency. There were also greater supplies of milk products from other markets, such as Denmark and overseas, which caused a decrease in prices.

Private merchants, interested only in immediate profits and possessing no capital for long-term investments, were unable to improve the quality of milk products. That this quality was low can be deduced from the fact that the butter bought up from the farmers had been prepared in a variety of ways, mostly by primitive methods. The butter was then mixed and packed for export. Naturally, prices for such "mixtures," were low, but eventually it became impossible to sell the product even at low prices.

The government was anxious to help the farmers by improving milk products and increasing exports. The best way to do that seemed to be by coöperation, a method which in later years fully justified the expectations. Through the initiative of the coöperatives and with government subsidies, the quality of butter was improved so much that in 1936, of all the butter-exporting countries, only Denmark was able to get higher prices than Lithuania. Lithuania's position in this market shows even more creditable progress when we

[33] *Centraline Lietuvos Pieno Perdirbimo Bendroviu Sajunga Pienocentras 1927–1936* (The Central Union of Dairy Coöperative Societies of Lithuania, Pienocentras, 1927–1936), p. 15.

take into consideration the fact that Danish butter had been selling in London for decades and the English consumers had acquired a taste for it.[34]

The first to organize the dairies were the Central Union of the Agricultural Coöperatives of Lithuania (Lietukis) and the Coöperative Society (Gamintojas). In 1923 a separate dairying section was established at Lietukis. The Ministry of Agriculture subsidized the newly organized steam

CHART I

BUTTER EXPORTS OF LITHUANIA

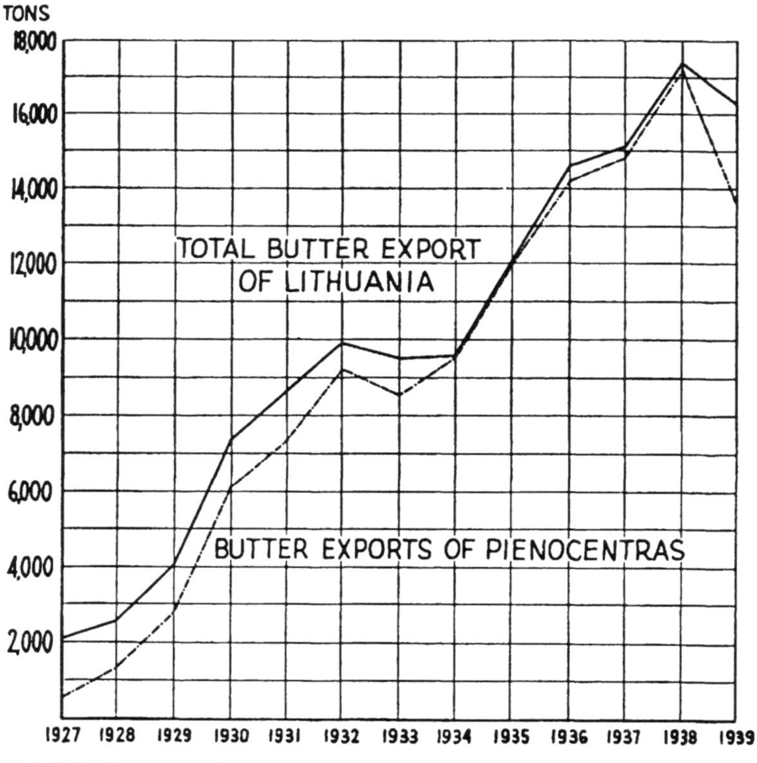

[34] Kriksciunas, *op. cit.*, p. 96.

dairies (using steam power equipment) to enable them to buy new machinery, granting the dairies twenty-five percent of the value of the machinery, the subsidy not to exceed 9,000 litas. Subsidies up to 1,500 litas were also given to hand dairies in the same percentage. The Ministry of Agriculture also provided loans on favorable terms for the construction of buildings for new dairies and from 1925 granted subsidies up to 5,000 litas for this purpose. In 1926 the dairying section of Lietukis was organized into a separate organization—the Central Union of Dairy Coöperative Societies of Lithuania, known by its trade name, Pienocentras. The growth of coöperative dairies is shown in Table 20.

TABLE 20

THE GROWTH OF COÖPERATIVE DAIRIES IN LITHUANIA[a]

YEAR	NUMBER OF DAIRIES	NUMBER OF SKIMMING STATIONS
1923	3	—
1924	61	—
1925	54	—
1927	153	151
1929	262	660
1931	273	1,610
1933	251	1,825
1935	209	1,771
1937	188	2,052
1938	185	2,105
1939	176	2,159

[a] *Centraline Lietuvos Pieno Perdirbimo Bendroviu Sajunga Pienocentras 1927–1936*, p. 21.

From 1931 the number of dairies decreased while the number of skimming stations increased. This is due to the fact that some of the dairies were converted into skimming stations because of insufficient machinery. There were many instances of the merging of several small dairies into one large dairy, while the other units were converted into skimming stations.[35] Simultaneously with the increase in the number of dairying establishments, the quantity of milk and butter products increased very substantially.

It will be noted that milk and butter production in the other two Baltic countries, Latvia and Estonia, increased slowly, remaining almost constant in the latter, while in Lith-

TABLE 21

PRODUCTION OF DAIRY PRODUCTS IN THE BALTIC STATES

MILK

(*1,000 Hectoliters*)

YEAR	LITHUANIA [a]	LATVIA	ESTONIA
1928	397	12,650	6,387
1929	725	13,143	6,334
1930	1,512	13,424	7,374
1931	1,910	13,948	7,866
1932	2,430	14,161	7,877
1933	2,321	14,423	7,673
1934	2,537	15,548	7,821
1935	3,057	15,713	7,929
1936	3,773	15,868	7,791
1937 [b]	4,074	16,179	8,134
1938 [c]	5,133	([f])	([f])
1939	6,250	([f])	([f])

[35] *Ibid.*, p. 90.

BUTTER

(*1,000 Metric Tons*)

YEAR	LITHUANIA [a]	LATVIA	ESTONIA
1928	1.6	14.3	12.2
1929	3.1	17.0	13.7
1930	6.4	20.8	15.5
1931	8.1	22.2	16.1
1932	10.3	22.1	14.5
1933	9.9	18.6	11.5
1934	10.7	18.8	12.6
1935	13.2	20.5	13.3
1936	15.8	22.2	13.8
1937 [d]	17.1	21.7	15.9
1938 [e]	19.6	([f])	([f])
1939	19.9	([f])	([f])

[a] Only milk controlled by dairies is included in this table.
[b] L.N. 1937–38, p. 72.
[c] C.S.B., volumes for 1938 and 1939.
[d] L.N., 1937–38, p. 74.
[e] C.S.B., volumes for 1938 and 1939.
[f] Figures not available.

uania production increased more than tenfold during the ten-year period. The chief cause for this is that dairying in Latvia and Estonia was considerably advanced before the World War, which was not the case in Lithuania. During the recent years, before the Soviet occupation, however, Lithuania not only succeeded in reaching Estonia's level of butter production but even surpassed it. This situation shows how retarded dairying was in Lithuania as compared with Latvia and Estonia, and indicates the great achievement of coöperation in this particular field.

The expansion of dairying in Lithuania may be observed also from export figures, given in Table 22.

TABLE 22

BUTTER EXPORTS IN THE BALTIC STATES[a]

(In Metric Tons)

YEAR	LITHUANIA	LATVIA	ESTONIA
1927	2,051	10,761	9,906
1928	2,643	13,006	11,222
1929	4,084	14,830	12,359
1930	7,357	13,430	14,066
1931	8,705	18,739	14,444
1932	9,926	18,598	12,531
1933	9,580	15,720	9,224
1934	9,671	15,701	10,118
1935	12,154	16,816	10,838
1936	14,629	17,291	10,955
1937	15,058	19,211	13,179
1938	17,413	23,464	14,732
1939	16,386	([b])	([b])

[a] C.S.B., volumes for 1927 to 1939.
[b] Figures not available.

LIVESTOCK

Livestock breeding is one of the branches of agriculture that suffered greatly in the World War. As soon as the war started in 1914 Russia requisitioned the best horses for the army. Then came the German army, which took what had been left by the Russians. Only horses unfit for army use were left.

To alleviate a great shortage of food caused by the Allied blockade the Germans requisitioned even the milk cows for slaughter. The reduction in livestock in Lithuania in 1919 as compared with 1913 was as follows: horses, 38 percent; cattle, 47.7 percent; pigs, 44 percent; sheep, 30 percent. The reduction of stock may be clearly seen from Table 23,

TABLE 23

LIVESTOCK IN LITHUANIA 1913–39

YEAR	HORSES (1,000 head)	CATTLE (1,000 head)	PIGS (1,000 head)	SHEEP (1,000 head)
1913	451	918	1,138	1,152
1919	280	480	750	806
1920	335	604	1,119	894
1921	376	780	1,262	1,036
1925	497	1,339	1,488	1,455
1928 [a]	611	1,128	1,010	1,409
1930	562	1,034	1,207	1,212
1935 [b]	545	1,132	1,223	1,220
1938 [c]	558	1,193	1,249	1,241
1939	521	1,004	1,117	1,224

[a] For the period 1913–28: Kubilius, *op. cit.*, p. 86; C.S.B., 1918–28, p. 58.
[b] For the years 1930 and 1935: *Lietuvos Surasymas*, 1935, pp. 40–51.
[c] C.S.B., volumes for 1938 and 1939.

which shows also that livestock breeding recovered very quickly after the World War, so that as early as 1925 the number of livestock was even greater than it had been in 1913. Exports of livestock and their products constituted 26.13 percent of the total value of exports as early as 1924 and reached 31.02 percent in 1928 and 61.4 percent in 1939. It may be interesting to analyze the livestock situation according to its various important branches.

Horses were bred in Lithuania as far back as historians can trace the Lithuanian people. That horses are beloved by Lithuanians is proved by the many folk songs about them. In the Middle Ages Lithuania needed horses for its wars and bred them in great numbers for that purpose. Some of them were even sold in foreign markets.[36]

[36] Krikscíunas, *op. cit.*, p. 152.

Table 24

EXPORT VALUE OF LIVESTOCK AND THEIR PRODUCTS[a]

(In Thousands of Litas)

YEAR	HORSES	CATTLE	PIGS	MEAT, MEAT PRODUCTS	MILK, BUTTER, CHEESE	SKINS	BRISTLES, HAIR, BONES	TOTAL	PERCENT OF NATION'S TOTAL EXPORTS
1924	16,219	5,404	11,773	10,966	6,969	16,022	4,233	71,586	26.1
1925	14,475	7,386	14,119	6,672	12,123	11,731	3,397	69,903	28.9
1926	5,322	9,320	20,895	8,641	16,295	7,123	3,067	70,663	28.4
1927	10,993	6,756	12,864	6,826	17,537	11,315	2,133	68,424	27.8
1928	9,820	7,445	11,533	5,874	25,560	17,160	2,186	79,578	31.0
1930	10,306	12,975	38,753	46,112	52,543	7,790	2,652	171,131	51.3
1935	3,435	106	7,084	25,808	24,878	3,286	1,149	65,746	43.2
1937	4,964	2,189	16,336	31,127	48,193	7,343	1,782	111,934	53.7
1938	5,060	2,837	21,257	36,196	58,110	5,569	1,454	130,483	55.9
1939	3,300	2,436	23,509	39,884	50,056	4,055	1,614	124,854	61.4

[a] C.S.B., volumes for 1924 to 1939.

In recent years horses have been used a great deal for farm work. Lithuania being a country of small farms, it is usually quite impossible for the farmer to invest in expensive machinery. Furthermore, labor is too cheap for mechanized farming to be able to compete with it. Thus, the total number of horses in Lithuania is considerably larger than in the neighboring countries, Latvia and Estonia.

Shortly before the World War, and immediately after it, the small "Samogitian horses" (Zemaitukai) or "Lithuanian horses" were especially famous in western Europe. They are unusually hardy and are of the same breed as those with which Lithuanians in the Middle Ages made their inroads into Smolensk, Novgorod, and Moscow in their wars with the Russians.[37] These horses are especially suited for use in a country of large forests, bad roads, and primitive farming. But at the end of the nineteenth century, and especially at the beginning of the twentieth, conditions changed. More advanced farming with heavier tools required bigger and stronger horses, and horses of this type were crossed with the small "Samogitians." At the present time there are found many breeds of horses, but very few are of a pure breed. After the World War horse raising was vastly improved by establishing free central stations for horse husbandry. The sturdy "Samogitians" were valuable particularly for work in mines.

Shortly after the World War, demand for horses being great and prices high, a substantial number of horses were exported, but in recent years the export of horses has been

[37] *Ibid.*, p. 153.

TABLE 25

EXPORT OF HORSES 1924–39

YEAR	NUMBER OF HORSES	VALUE (In million litas)
1924	23,204	16.2
1926	10,347	5.3
1928	27,224	9.8
1930	20,647	10.3
1932	8,215	2.2
1934	17,318	4.6
1936	14,900	5.6
1937	13,262	4.9
1938	12,230	5.1
1939	7,130	3.3

on the decline. The greatest importers of Lithuanian horses are Latvia, the Netherlands, Denmark, and Finland. In 1938 the export of Lithuanian horses was as follows:

Latvia	3,254	Belgium	1,041	Germany	378
Netherlands	2,284	Switzerland	837	Czechoslovakia	37
Denmark	1,908	Sweden	698	Estonia	6
Finland	1,277	Great Britain	341		

Cattle breeding is one of the branches of livestock husbandry which not only recovered rapidly from the ravages of the World War but showed both a slight increase in number of head as compared with 1913 and a substantial improvement in quality. Evidence of improved quality is shown by the tenfold increase in butter production. The 1930 and 1935 censuses reveal the various categories of Lithuanian cattle as in Table 26.

TABLE 26

CATEGORIES OF LITHUANIAN CATTLE IN 1930 AND 1935[a]

	1930	1935
Calves less than one year old	216,890	160,670
Heifers one year old and older	135,670	176,300
Oxen one year old and older	27,200	38,730
Milk cows	654,030	755,830
TOTAL	1,033,790	1,131,530

[a] *Lietuvos Surasymas,* 1935, pp. 43–44.

From this table we see that about 65 percent of all the cattle of Lithuania are milk cows. The total number of cattle increased in 1935 as compared with 1930 by 9.5 percent, while the number of calves less than a year old was substantially smaller.

Pig breeding, another important branch of Lithuanian agriculture, is connected to some extent with dairying. This is because the dairies yield large quantities of skimmed milk, which is always an excellent feed for pigs. Until 1924 the exports of pigs and pork from Lithuania were insignificant, but in later years, especially since 1930, after the Maistas Corporation developed its activities on a wider scale, the exports have increased considerably. In its stockyard at Kaunas about 800 workers were employed before the Russian occupation, while in the establishments at Siauliai, Panevezys and Taurage, smaller numbers were employed.

Sheep breeding in Lithuania is mainly for wool production, but wool has not played any great role in the exports of Lithuania, as the bulk was consumed by domestic agriculturists for making cloth at home. After the World War, conditions gradually changed; the farmers began to sell sur-

TABLE 27

EXPORT OF PIGS AND PORK PRODUCTS 1924–39

YEAR	LIVE PIGS (*1,000 head*)	BACON	FRESH PORK
		(*1,000 metric tons*) [a]	
1924	43.5	0.0	1.1
1926	72.0	0.0	2.0
1928	41.8	0.6	1.2
1930	154.1	17.4	3.2
1932	33.7	40.9	5.5
1934	46.1	30.7	4.4
1936	117.0	10.2	5.1
1937	137.7	10.5	3.5
1938	153.1	11.8	1.6
1939	179.7	15.6	1.1

[a] One metric ton = 2,204.6 U.S. pounds.

plus wool and to buy clothing ready-made in town instead of making it themselves. Since the climate is unfavorable for sheep breeding and the wool from Lithuanian sheep is therefore poor, domestic wool is mixed by the textile industry of Lithuania with imported wool of better quality. The value of wool imports in recent years was as follows: in 1936, 1,859,700 litas; in 1937, 2,558,900 litas; in 1938, 1,681,900 litas and in 1939 1,436,100 litas. The bulk of this wool came from Great Britain. There is perhaps no great future for sheep breeding; on the contrary, it is likely that this branch of livestock production will decrease even more.

POULTRY FARMING

Poultry farming is also a very old branch of Lithuania's agriculture, and the role it has played in the exports picture has not been unimportant. Poultry farming is especially suited to countries with small farms, but in Lithuania, compared with Belgium, Holland, and Denmark, it is still undeveloped.[38]

TABLE 28

POULTRY PRODUCTION IN 1935[a]

FOWL	NUMBER	PERCENTAGE OF ENTIRE POULTRY PRODUCTION
Hens	4,614,420	72.4
Ducks	601,450	9.4
Geese	946,510	14.9
Turkeys	210,730	3.3

[a] *Lietuvos Surasymas*, 1935, p. 51.

In the first years of independent Lithuania, egg production, in comparison with the production in other branches of agriculture, was high, but in later years it diminished in importance and relinquished its position to milk products and meat. The highest prices for eggs exported were received in 1921–22. In the latter year, egg exports constituted almost a third of the whole export value, as may be seen from Table 29. The main cause of the decrease in exports of eggs after 1922 was, of course, the fall in prices. In 1922 the

TABLE 29

MAIN EXPORT ITEMS OF LITHUANIA 1920–22

	1920	1921	1922
Total value of exports (in millions of marks)	490	631	3,047
Flax (percent of total)	46.4	29.3	7.8
Forest products (percent)	35.5	30.3	39.0
Eggs (percent)	3.6	23.4	32.1

[38] Krikściunas, *op. cit.*, p. 85.

wholesale price for ten eggs in London was 4.90 litas; in 1923, 4.19 litas; in 1922, 3.73 litas; and in 1927, 2.45 litas.[39] From Table 29 it may be seen that in the first years of Lithuanian's independent national existence the most important exports were forest products, flax, and eggs; in later years, when conditions became more settled, these products became of secondary importance. How poultry production and poultry exports changed in value after 1924 may be seen from Table 30. The exports of eggs did not diminish in volume as much as in value, because the most drastic

TABLE 30

EXPORTS OF POULTRY AND POULTRY PRODUCTS

(In Thousands of Litas)

YEAR	EGGS	POULTRY [a]	POULTRY MEATS	TOTAL
1924	19,938	4,956	391	24,285
1925	14,872	3,824	308	19,003
1926	13,575	5,206	817	19,597
1927	10,944	4,511	560	16,015
1928	14,435	6,810	157	21,393
1930	11,892	7,759	1,806	21,457
1935	2,117	1	1,369	3,487
1938	7,833	2,283	2,746	12,862
1939	8,196	3,170	3,615	14,981

[a] Geese, hens, ducks, turkeys.

drop in price levels occurred in 1931–32. For a few years before the Soviet Russian occupation experiments were conducted in the improvement of poultry and in the organizing of efficient egg-collection stations. This was done by the coöperatives. At the same time there was considerable improvement in the prices received for these products.

[39] Kubilius, *op. cit.*, pp. 180–90.

Chapter III

INDUSTRY

The industry of Lithuania before the World War was governed not by the requirements of the local markets. Its development and structure were more suited to the Russian empire, on whose national economy, politics, and markets Lithuania was dependent. There was extensive development of such industries as leather and metal, which had no basic connections with the markets of ethnographic Lithuania. At the same time, industries closely connected with agriculture were almost nonexistent. There were no slaughterhouses where the livestock surplus could be prepared for export, and there was almost no textile industry; the country's flax had to go to western Europe for manufacture into cloth. Even the timber industry, which was in a very favorable situation, was undeveloped. This same industry was flourishing just across the border, in the port of Klaipeda (Memel) in pre-World War Germany, although it was wholly dependent for its raw materials on Lithuania and the rest of pre-war Russia.[1]

After the World War the remnants of the Russian industries in Lithuania were unsuited to the needs of the newly established republic. And even those remnants were almost completely disabled, because during the hostilities the ma-

[1] C.S.B., 1918–28, pp. 67–90.

chinery had been destroyed or sent to "unknown destinations." Therefore the industry of the reëstablished republic had not only to be reconstructed but had to be almost entirely reshaped in a manner suited to the needs of an agricultural country. According to the vague pre-World War statistics, there were approximately 3,144 separate industrial units in Lithuania, this number including very small establishments of three to five workers. According to statistics compiled from reports of factory inspectors,[2] the province (gouvernement) of Kaunas had 151 enterprises with 6,603 workers, distributed as in Table 31.

TABLE 31

INDUSTRY OF LITHUANIA IN 1913

NUMBER OF ENTERPRISES	NUMBER OF WORKERS IN EACH
1	1,256
2	600
2	200
2	100–200
12	51–100
7	31–50
13	21–30
34	11–30
78	less than 10

After the World War the leather and metal industries experienced a great setback, while the food, textile, paper, and other industries soon started on the upswing. An idea of the rapid increase in the number of industrial establishments may be gained from the number of government operation certificates issued. In 1920, 2,474 certificates were issued;

[2] Kubilius, *op. cit.*, pp. 222–23.

in 1921, 4,011; in 1922, 4,933; in 1923, 5,402; in 1924, 5,419; in 1925, 5,941; in 1926, 5,164; in 1927, 5,437; in 1928, 5,742; in 1929, 6,010; in 1930, 5,842; in 1931, 5,796; in 1932, 5,735; in 1933, 5,451; in 1934, 5,710; in 1935, 12,067; in 1936, 14,750; in 1937, 15,214; in 1938, 15,717; and in 1939, 16,131.[3]

The sudden rise of the number of industrial establishments registered in 1935 and the subsequent years is the result of the extension of the License Tax in that year to even the smallest establishments. The new ruling required that a license be taken out even by concerns with only a single employee. Thus the figures of 1935 and later are not wholly comparable with the previous ones; nevertheless they reflect the rise of industry in Lithuania. A more detailed picture of the development of industry may be obtained from Table 32, which shows that the largest number, over 20 percent, of wage earners are employed in the textile industry. The food and luxury goods industries, which in 1937 held third position with 5,195 employees, advanced to second place in 1938, with 6,150 workers. The third place in 1938 was held by the timber industry, with 4,852 workers, having enjoyed during the previous year an all-time peak in its record of employment. Fourth place, according to the number of workers employed, belongs to the clay products and stone industry; after it come the metals and machinery industry and the clothing and footwear industry.

When the value of industrial production is taken into consideration we get a very different picture of the situation, with the food and luxury industry in first place, accounting for over 41 percent of the total value of the industrial production of Lithuania. Next follow the textile

[3] C.S.B., 1938 and 1939, p. 186 and p. 194 respectively.

Table 32

CLASSIFICATION OF INDUSTRIAL ESTABLISHMENTS OF LITHUANIA 1927–39[a]

INDUSTRY	1927		1930		1935		1938		1939[b]	
	Establish-ments	*Employees*	*Establish-ments*	*Employees*	*Establish-ments*	*Employees*	*Establish-ments*	*Employees*	*Establish-ments*	*Employees*
Peat-cutting	7	603	6	541	7	417	16	1,086	19	1,296
Stone, clay products, etc.	94	1,357	108	1,648	82	1,539	130	3,566	130	3,212
Metals and machinery	97	1,895	94	1,975	92	1,711	120	3,327	97	2,981
Chemicals	49	885	53	792	48	940	48	1,583	53	1,695
Leather and fur	40	657	44	648	37	749	58	1,022	50	865
Textiles	55	1,403	57	2,194	61	4,679	81	7,019	84	4,611[c]
Timber	185	3,446	178	3,096	192	4,238	264	4,852	238	2,864[d]
Paper and printing	52	2,115	64	2,323	71	2,195	84	2,615	81	1,613[e]
Foodstuffs	253	3,786	246	3,616	343	4,284	394	6,150	347	5,925
Clothing and footwear	139	1,607	154	1,891	148	1,952	183	3,056	186	2,841
Electricity and gas works	29	648	26	479	31	512	33	590	31	474

[a] C.S.B., *Statistikos Metrastis*, Vol. 1929–39.
[b] All data in this column after seizure of Klaipeda Territory by Germany in March, 1939.
[c] Before Klaipeda Territory cession: 87 establishments with 7,561 employees.
[d] Before Klaipeda Territory cession: 206 establishments with 4,257 employees.
[e] Before Klaipeda Territory cession: 88 establishments with 2,679 employees.

industry with 14.9 percent, the timber industry—9.1 percent, and the paper and printing industry—8.4 percent. These facts may be clearly seen from Table 33, which shows

TABLE 33

AGGREGATE VALUE OF INDUSTRIAL PRODUCTION OF LITHUANIA 1937–39

(In Thousands of Litas)

INDUSTRY	1937	1938	1939
Peat-cutting	1,277	1,873	2,932
Stone, clay products, etc.	7,012	9,097	9,389
Metals and machinery	19,298	24,661	23,378
Chemicals	13,939	16,529	20,734
Leather and fur	17,245	16,684	14,306
Textiles	35,656	40,331	40,331
Timber	15,847	16,865	14,341
Paper and printing	17,807	17,543	17,630
Food and luxury goods	151,569	175,470	223,424
Clothing and footwear	20,762	23,658	26,696
Electrical works	10,672	11,738	12,588
TOTAL	311,084	354,449	405,749

that the value of total production in 1939 was 405,749,000 litas against 354,449,000 litas in 1938 and 311,084,000 litas in 1937.

The growth of the industrial production of Lithuania was not even impaired by the world depression of 1929. While world production in 1931 and 1932 had fallen to the lowest ebb, production in Lithuania showed further expansion. Several reasons may be given in explanation of this phenomenon.

First, Lithuania exercises a specific customs duties system, which is an advantage to home industry during a period of

TABLE 34

INDUSTRIAL PRODUCTION INDEX OF LITHUANIA AND THE WORLD 1929–39

YEAR	PRODUCTION OF LITHUANIA [a]	WORLD PRODUCTION [b]
1929	100	100
1930	108.3	88.3
1931	140.7	74.8
1932	153.7	63.0
1933	([d])	71.3
1934	166.5	77.0
1935	185.9	85.4
1936	244.2	95.5
1937	272.0	102.5
1938	309.4	125.8 [c]
1939	354.2	128.7

[a] *Report*, p. 20.
[b] League of Nations, *Monthly Bulletin of Statistics*, Geneva, June, 1938.
[c] *Ibid., Statistical Year-Book 1939–40.*
[d] Figure not available.

falling prices in the world market, especially when the duties are high as compared with the prices of commodities. Customs duties do not fall in proportion to the fall of prices in the world market, as would be the case under the ad valorem duties system. Thus, home industry benefited from the fall of raw-material prices and was able to supply the home market with cheaper commodities than could be offered by the foreign producers for whose products the customs duties were not lowered to suit the decreased prices. This is proved even by the great decrease in the value of imports, which in 1935 amounted to only 128,597,000 litas, as against 142,-176,200 litas in 1933 and 312,415,200 in 1930.

Second, it is to be noted that the index of industrial production did not suffer as much in the agricultural countries as it did in advanced industrial countries. For example, the index of the industrial production of Germany in 1929 fell from 100 to 85.9 in 1930, to 67.6 in 1931, and to 53.3 in 1932. The index of the United States was 80.7 in 1930, 68.1 in 1931, and 53.8 in 1932. At the same time, the index number of the industrial production of Denmark was below 100 only in 1932, when it was 91, while in 1933 it was 105 and in 1934, 117. The index number of the industrial production of Greece continued to stay over 100: in 1930 it was 103.4; in 1931, 107.0; and in 1932, 100.9, while in 1938 it reached 165.1.[4]

Finally, the industry of Lithuania, even with expanded facilities, does not satisfy the demands of its home market. For this reason even during the depression the rate of industrial expansion was not greatly slackened.

Aside from coöperative concerns, analysis of which has been made elsewhere, a great role in the economic life of Lithuania was played by corporations.

In some of them, as in the Maistas and Lietuvos Cukrus corporations, the majority of stock is held by the government.

At the end of 1939 there were 137 corporations in Lithuania with total capitalization of 205,442,000 litas. The banking group comprised 8 units with total capitalization of 89,000,000 litas or 43 percent of total capital of the corporations of Lithuania. Next in importance comes food industry with 20 corporations and 28,345,000 litas combined capital followed by 4 electricity supply corporations with 25,100,000 litas of capital stock.

[4] League of Nations, *Statistical Year-Book 1939–40.*

With the Sovietization of Lithuania by Russia all those corporations were nationalized in August, 1940, and made government establishments. On August 7, 1940, an order was published requesting even the surrender of the shares of capital stock and bonds of private corporations or government.[5] No due compensation was promised.

When Russian occupation was substituted by German in June, 1941, the system of private ownership was returned in Lithuania, except private, corporate, or coöperative wealth, which apparently is kept for distribution to German nationals or at least to German sympathizers.

THE TEXTILE INDUSTRY

The textile industry showed a spectacular rise between 1927 and 1940. But even before this period it had shown considerable advance. It is estimated that in the years 1909 to 1913 this industry in Lithuania employed about 300 workers.[6] In 1927 the number of workers had grown to 1,403, almost five times as many as before the World War, while in 1939 the industry was employing 7,561 workers.

It is interesting to note that in spite of increasing textile production at home, imports did not decrease proportionately. This may be accounted for partly by the fact that rising living standards increased the demand to such an extent that even the increased production was not sufficient to satisfy it without the aid of proportionately high imports. Lithuania does not export any textile fabrics.

The expanding textile industry modifies the type of textile

[5] *Darbo Lietuva* No. 50, Aug. 13, 1940. (*Darbo Lietuva* [Worker's Lithuania] was a Bolshevik daily in Kaunas, established after the occupation.)

[6] L.G.S.A., 1937, p. 405.

TABLE 35

THE DEVELOPMENT OF THE TEXTILE INDUSTRY OF LITHUANIA 1927–39

KIND OF ESTAB-LISHMENT	1927		1930		1935		1939	
	Estab-lish-ments	*Work-ers*	*Estab-lish-ments*	*Work-ers*	*Estab-lish-ments*	*Work-ers*	*Estab-lish-ments*	*Work-ers*
Linen and jute weaving	3	112	3	163	5	624	5	827
Flax preparation	16	468	9	534	8	288	11	1,296
Woolen and cotton weaving and spinning	6	589	7	1,229	16	2,922	20	4,051
Wool spinning	17	138	20	142	11	67	23	175
Silk weaving	—	—	—	—	3	651	4	964

imports: there is a tendency toward an increase in semifinished textile goods, especially woolen spun yarns, and a decrease in imports of woolen textile materials (fabrics). In cotton-goods imports this tendency is not so pronounced. This may be due partly to the fact that Lithuania has no raw cotton and the entire supply must be imported. The manufacturing of cotton fabrics is, therefore, almost entirely undeveloped. With woolen fabrics conditions are exactly opposite. A substantial part of the wool is produced at home and, although the quality of Lithuanian wool is not as high as that of Australia or New Zealand, the woolen industries, having been at first wholly dependent on the home supply, were better equipped to expand and improve their production than were the cotton factories. If breeds of sheep are improved as were those of cattle, Lithuanian woolen goods will improve in quality as well as increase in quantity.

TABLE 36

IMPORTS OF THE LEADING SEMIFINISHED AND FINISHED TEXTILE GOODS

(In Thousands of Litas)

YEAR	WOOLEN SPUN YARN	COTTON SPUN YARN	WOOLEN FABRICS	COTTON FABRICS	TOTAL
1928	2,188	6,032	12,952	21,118	42,291
1929	2,413	7,449	14,179	18,600	42,643
1930	2,269	12,019	16,543	21,867	52,699
1931	2,576	8,801	14,980	24,082	50,439
1932	2,034	7,916	7,319	11,370	28,639
1933	3,264	8,917	4,430	8,320	24,931
1934	4,334	7,951	3,717	7,132	23,133
1935	4,173	7,364	3,742	7,271	22,550
1936	7,061	8,662	5,067	10,230	31,020
1937	8,433	8,558	5,795	10,213	32,999
1938	8,433	7,761	5,299	9,536	31,029
1939	5,004	5,499	4,564	8,654	23,721

FOODSTUFFS INDUSTRY

Among Lithuanian industries, foodstuffs occupied first place (41.6%) from the point of view of value of product in 1937 and second place from the point of view of number of people employed. From 1927 to 1938 this branch of industry almost doubled in number of employees. Table 37 shows this expansion. The meat, fish, and canned goods branch showed an exceptional rise. In 1939 the number of workers rose to 1,987 or more than five times the number (362) employed in 1927. The Maistas Corporation, with its five stockyards (Kaunas, Klaipeda, Siauliai, Panevezys, and Taurage), has been responsible for most of this progress.

The Maistas Corporation was originally organized in 1923

TABLE 37

THE FOODSTUFFS INDUSTRIES

INDUSTRY	1927		1930		1935		1938		1939	
	Establish-ments	*Employees*	*Establish-ments*	*Employees*	*Establish-ments*	*Employees*	*Establish-ments*	*Employees*	*Establish-ments*	*Employees*
Grain mills	83	778	74	638	83	619	99	761	96	706
Bakeries	21	156	29	212	43	319	53	465	46	469
Sugar refin-eries	—	—	—	—	1	133	2	262	2	246
Candy and chocolate factories	40	760	42	866	29	583	36	761	28	657
Slaughter-houses and meat, fish, and canned goods estab-lishments	20	362	20	281	21	1,029	25	1,721	15	1,787 [a]
Milk-prod-uct plants	4	26	18	114	110	407	114	507	102	458
Breweries	10	350	10	351	10	246	11	602	9	553
Tobacco and cigarette factories	12	734	10	695	9	574	8	569	6	546

[a] Before Klaipeda Territory cession: 26 establishments with 1,987 workers.

for the purpose of concentrating on the export of eggs and dairy products, but later its activities were turned to organizing slaughterhouses and to producing and exporting meat and canned products.[7] The original capital of the Maistas Corporation was 500,000 litas, consisting of 5,000 shares at 100 litas par value. The first years of the corporation were not only nonprosperous, but the balance for July 1, 1924, showed a loss of 463,237.60 litas. This loss was covered by stockholders in proportional payments according to the stock

[7] *Pirmas Maisto Desimtmetis 1923–1933 Metai* (Maistas's First Decade, 1923–1933), Kaunas, 1933, p. 28.

held. The first loss did not discourage the promoters, however. In 1925 the capital stock of the corporation was raised to 10,000,000 litas. This increase was motivated by the fact that in constructing the first stockyard the corporation had indebted itself to this amount. But even then the prospects of the corporation were not very encouraging. Private owners soon sought to rid themselves of the stock held, which at the end of 1925 was absorbed by such important organizations as the Union of Farmers of Lithuania, 2,250 shares; the Union of Agricultural Coöperative Societies of Lithuania (Lietukis), 2,000 shares; the coöperative society Lietuvos Eksimportas, 670 shares; and by many smaller units subscribing to their proportionate number of shares. Thus the Maistas Corporation, having been founded as a strictly private enterprise, became an important public enterprise. In March of 1930 the by-laws of the corporation were changed to comply with the new laws of the state and on March 22, 1930, the company was newly incorporated. In the same year the government of Lithuania purchased part of the stock of the corporation for 3,000,000 litas and later an additional portion for 4,000,000 litas. The Maistas Corporation therefore became an institution known in English-speaking countries as a mixed enterprise, from the point of view of control. In 1938, as has already been stated, it owned five stockyards in the most important cities of Lithuania. Its meat and livestock export rose from 226,106 litas in 1923 to 35,420,949 litas in 1932 and 42,720,000 litas in 1936, the last amount representing 22.4 percent of the total value of the country's exports.[8]

The organization showed an exceptionally spectacular rise in exports in the last two years before Soviet Russian occu-

[8] Kriksciunas, *op. cit.*, p. 151.

pation. In 1938, Maistas sales to foreign countries rose to 57.85 million litas, while in 1939 it rose to 71.7 million litas, or 24 percent above the 1938 figures.

Even in domestic business Maistas showed an impressive rise. Its domestic sales amounted in 1930 to 5.8 million litas and rose every subsequent year until in 1938 they reached 14.9 million litas and in 1939, 18.8 million litas.

The sugar industry, which also shows considerable advance, started with one refinery in 1932, employing 67 persons, and in 1939 had two refineries with 246 workers, not counting the many farmers who were engaged in sugar-beet growing and whose incomes were increased through the introduction and development of this branch of agriculture. Inasmuch as the two refineries were insufficient to meet the demands of Lithuania, a third refinery was constructed. All three are owned by the Lietuvos Cukrus Corporation, in which the government participates as owner of a controlling number of shares of capital stock. The first refinery was opened in 1932 in Marijampole and the second in 1935 in Panevezys. The production rose very rapidly: in 1932, 67,000 quintals; 1933, 162,000 quintals; 1934, 82,000 quintals; 1935, 153,000 quintals; 1936, 221,000 quintals; 1937, 272,000 quintals; in 1938, 287,000 quintals [9] and 1939, 208,000 quintals.

Another industry in the food-and-luxury category which showed great expansion both in number of establishments and in workers employed is that of dairying, which is covered in the section on coöperatives, above.

Other industries, such as grain mills with 761 workers, candy and chocolate factories with 761 workers, and tobacco

[9] C.S.B., 1938, p. 160.

and cigarette factories with 569 workers, continued to operate at about the same level throughout these past years.

LUMBER INDUSTRY

Some understanding of the lumber industry may be obtained from Table 38.[10] It will be observed that sawmilling

TABLE 38

LUMBER INDUSTRY

BRANCH OF INDUSTRY	1927		1930		1935		1938		1939[a]	
	Establishments	Workers	Establishments	Workers	Establishments	Workers	Establishments	Workers	Establishments	Workers
Sawmilling	131	2,731	114	1,718	124	2,853	175	2,970	170	1,901
Plywood production	—	—	3	443	3	602	3	767	1	27
Cabinet-making	6	90	10	229	8	251	88	963	61	839

[a] After seizure of Klaipeda by Germany.

is the leading branch of the lumber industry, although it does not show great expansion. The same may be said of the plywood industry. The latter felt the greatest setback with the loss of Klaipeda. The lumber industry, producing mainly for export, was hit by the world depression more severely than any other industry.

Before the agricultural products industry was developed for export, lumber was one of the most important items exported from Lithuania. It is to be noted that with the ex-

[10] C.S.B., 1938 and 1939, pp. 170–71 and 160–61 respectively.

pansion of the lumber industry the exported products changed. In 1920 69.1 percent of lumber was exported as raw material as against 30.9 percent semifinished items, while in 1921 this percentage changed to 49.9 percent raw as against 50.1 percent semifinished.

In 1939 this industry experienced a severe blow with the seizure of Klaipeda by Germany, the industry having been concentrated in Klaipeda. With the return of the Vilnius region to Lithuania at the end of 1939, the lumber industry was compensated somewhat, but to what extent it was impossible to establish, since seven months later came the Soviet Russian occupation.

PAPER AND PRINTING INDUSTRY

The paper and printing industry of Lithuania in 1938 employed 2,615 wage earners and accounted for 8.4 percent of the gross value of Lithuania's industrial production and 10.8 percent of the net value. Therefore, from the standpoint both of the number of wage earners employed and of the value of production, it was in the fourth place. Like the lumber industry, it suffered in 1939 when Germany seized Klaipeda where several of the larger printing establishments were located. Before the German occupation of Klaipeda, Lithuania had 88 establishments with 2,679 workers, while thereafter she had 81 establishments with 1,613 workers.[11]

From the statistics available it may be seen that in 1913 this branch of industry was only in its infancy. In that year there were only 20 establishments with 284 wage earners in the province (gouvernement) of Kaunas, while in 1927, in the same region, there were 52 establishments with 2,115 wage earners. The industry reached its high point in 1930,

[11] C.S.B., 1938 and 1939, pp. 170–71 and 160–61 respectively.

when it had 64 establishments and employed 2,323 workers.

As the world depression of 1929 affected Lithuania much later than it did the more advanced industrial countries, the setback in this branch of industry was not felt until 1931, when the number of establishments decreased to 61 and the number of wage earners to 2,157. The all-time low was reached in 1932 when only 1,924 persons were employed. The next year a slight revival was felt and from that year the industry was on the upswing until in the beginning of 1939 it reached an all-time peak with 88 establishments and 2,679 wage earners.

The chief branch of the paper and printing industry is that of woodpulp and paper production. Although this branch is represented by only five establishments, it is greatest from the standpoint of number of workers employed: it accounts for from 40 to 45 percent of all workers in the paper and printing industry. The number employed in woodpulp and paper production was almost the same in 1938 as in 1927—1,159 and 1,133 respectively—although in 1932 it had dropped to 688. The production of woodpulp as well as paper and cardboard has increased very substantially since 1931.

The printing branch of the industry also showed considerable expansion. In 1927 there were 33 printing establishments, with 658 wage earners. By 1938 the industry had 51 printing establishments and 1,153 wage earners and in 1939, 50 establishments with 843 wage earners. Even the depression of 1929 did not greatly affect this branch of industry. Except for a slight setback in 1934 and in 1935, in which years the number of employed decreased to 801 and 777 respectively, the printing business continued to grow.

The other two divisions of the paper and printing industry, cardboard manufacturing and bookbinding, have a large number of establishments, but account for only about 15 percent of all the workers.

Chapter IV

FOREIGN TRADE

The customs boundaries and customs tariffs of Lithuania were established in May, 1919, from which time the statistics on foreign trade were compiled. But up to 1923 these statistics were such that the figures are not exactly comparable with those of the later years. The unstable German *Obost* and *Reichsmark* currency, which circulated in Lithuania up to the end of 1922 when the Lithuanian litas currency was introduced, may be regarded among the chief causes for this situation.

It will be noted from Table 39 that the value of foreign trade increased until 1930 when it reached an all-time high of 333,739,000 litas in exports and 312,415,000 in imports. If the year 1923 is taken as a base, with the index number 100 for imports and exports, the index number for exports of 1930 is 227 and for imports 199.

From 1930 foreign trade decreased, the lowest point for exports being reached in 1934 with the index number 100, and for imports in 1935, with the index number at 82. Full revival of foreign trade began in 1936 when the index number for exports was 130 and for imports 100. In 1938 it rose as high as 159 for exports and 143 for imports.

In analyzing these figures it must be recalled that the litas currency of Lithuania held its original gold parity and there was no devaluation up to the Soviet invasion in 1940.

VALUE OF FOREIGN TRADE

Table 39

VALUE OF IMPORTS AND EXPORTS

(In Thousands of Litas)

YEAR	EXPORTS	IMPORTS	DIFFERENCE
1923	146,795	156,627	— 9,832
1924	266,584	206,534	+60,040
1925	242,715	252,703	— 9,988
1926	253,300	240,761	+12,539
1927	245,929	265,694	—19,765
1928	256,881	291,091	—34,210
1929	329,842	306,422	+23,420
1930	333,739	312,415	+21,324
1931	273,119	277,959	— 4,840
1932	189,126	166,954	+22,172
1933	160,227	142,176	+18,051
1934	147,245	138,690	+ 8,555
1935	152,269	128,579	+23,689
1936	190,485	156,061	+34,424
1937	208,325	212,667	— 4,342
1938	233,198	223,686	+ 9,512
1939	203,194	169,362	+39,832

If the value of imports and exports, commencing with 1932, is translated into dollar currency, a very different index number is obtained. For example, the exchange rate of the litas in January, 1932, was 10.02 litas for $1.00; in January, 1934, 6.42 litas for $1.00; and in 1935, 5.99 litas for $1.00.[1]

It is interesting to note that in 1924 Lithuania had a very favorable trade balance, with exports exceeding imports by over 60 million litas. Three years later the position was ex-

[1] See Apendix F, Foreign Exchange Quotations in Kaunas.

actly opposite. Starting with 1927 the trade balance for two successive years was unfavorable. In 1927 imports exceeded exports by 19,764,700 litas and in 1928 by 34,210,100 litas. One of the chief causes for this condition may be found in the fact that in 1924 the prices for agricultural products were high, while in 1927 and 1928 they were substantially lower. As Table 39 shows, the trade balance of Lithuania is generally favorable.

SHIFTING OF THE COMMODITIES INVOLVED IN FOREIGN TRADE

One of the most interesting things in the foreign trade of Lithuania and one that also shows clearly which way the economic life of Lithuania is going is the shifting of commodities involved. In 1920 the chief exports of Lithuania were lumber and other forest products, which accounted for 40 percent; flax, which accounted for 34.3 percent; linseed, 12.2 percent; eggs, 3.7 percent; and livestock, 1.5 percent. No butter was exported in that year, and food exports generally played a very small role. In the next three years, 1921, 1922, and 1923, the export picture was somewhat changed. Although forest products still retained the most important position, eggs became one of the leading export commodities and in 1921 accounted for 23.5 percent of total exports; in 1922, 20.2 percent; and in 1923, 10.3 percent. But the rise in this commodity proved to be only temporary. In 1927 eggs were down to 4.4 percent of the total value of exports. At the same time there was a constant increase in livestock exports, which rose to 16.2 percent in 1926 [2] and to 21 percent in 1930. After 1925 the statistics of exports of Lithuania were divided into five groups: (1) the livestock group,

[2] C.S.B., *Lietuva Skaitmenimis 1918–1928,* pp. 91–126.

comprising horses, cattle, domestic and wild animals, and live poultry; (2) the food products group, comprising various kinds of meat, including poultry, dairy products, eggs, fish, grain, vegetables, sugar, liquors, and so forth; (3) the raw and semifinished goods, which consists of raw furs and skins, wool, various livestock products, plants, fodder, tim-

CHART II

CHANGE IN EXPORTS FROM LITHUANIA

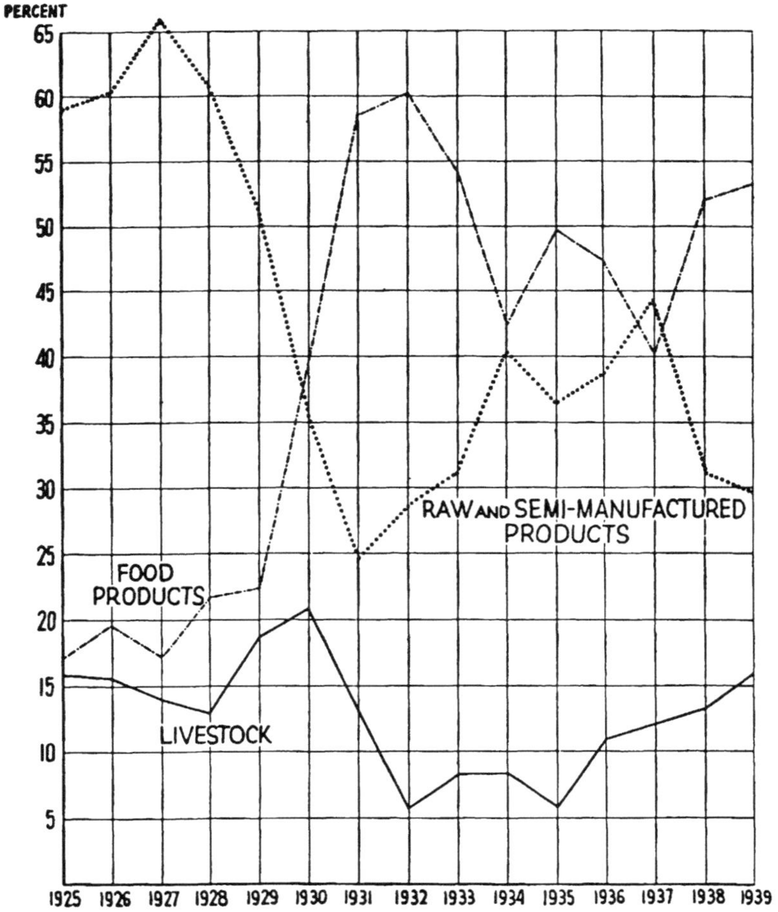

ber, forest products, woodpulp, rags, and so on; (4) the manufactured goods group, comprising cosmetics, paints, medicines, dressed furs and skins, spun yarn, tobacco, cigars and cigarettes, underwear, woodcraft products, paper and paper products, ceramics, machinery, and so on; (5) gold and silver.

CHART III

CHANGE IN IMPORTS INTO LITHUANIA

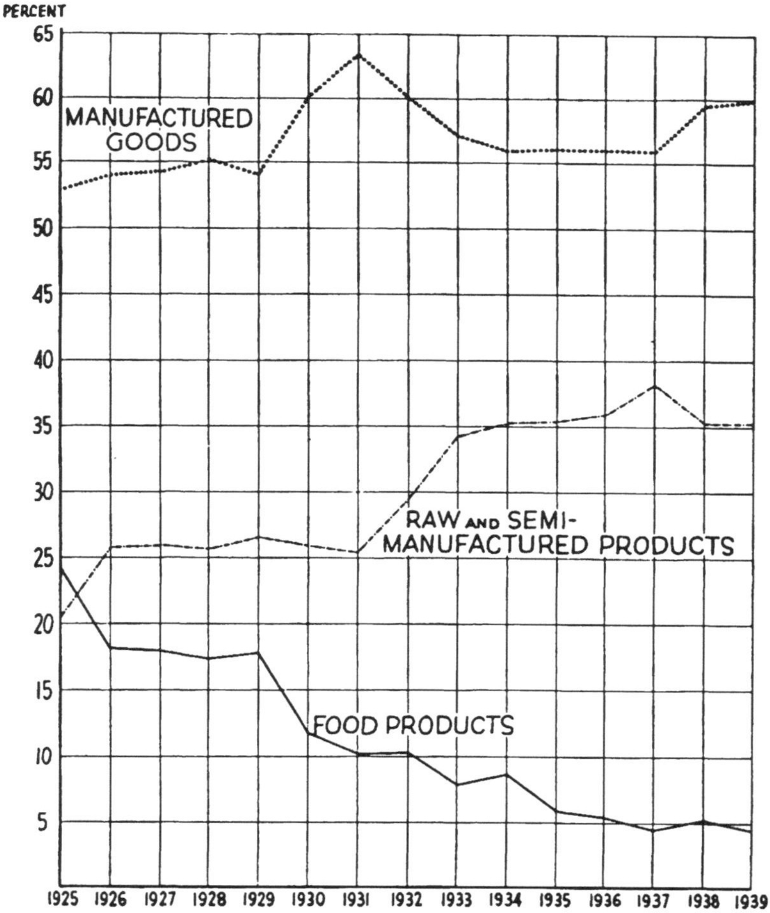

How the relative importance of these merchandise groups changed in Lithuania's export picture may be seen from Table 40, in which the figures show the percentage that each group bears to the total value of exports.[8] From this

TABLE 40

SHIFTING OF COMMODITY GROUPS IN EXPORTS 1925–39

(*Percent*)

YEAR	LIVESTOCK	FOOD PRODUCTS	RAW AND SEMIFINISHED PRODUCTS	FINISHED GOODS	GOLD AND SILVER
1925	16.56	17.12	59.27	6.96	0.09
1926	16.17	19.77	60.36	3.70	0.00
1927	14.33	17.38	66.10	2.13	0.06
1928	13.61	21.88	61.78	2.67	0.06
1929	18.83	22.72	51.55	6.85	0.05
1930	20.99	39.40	35.82	3.77	0.00
1931	13.13	57.38	24.56	4.92	0.01
1932	6.66	60.16	28.28	4.89	0.01
1933	8.36	54.19	31.49	5.94	0.00
1934	8.46	42.80	40.70	8.03	0.01
1935	6.98	49.53	36.98	6.48	0.03
1936	11.02	47.36	38.09	3.52	0.01
1937	12.02	40.17	44.14	3.67	—
1938	13.48	52.33	31.49	2.69	0.01
1939	16.13	53.04	29.80	1.02	0.01

table we see that from 1925 to 1939 the value of the exports in the food products group increased from 17.12 to 53.04 percent, while the group of raw and semifinished products decreased from 59.26 to 29.80 percent. The livestock and manufactured goods groups showed great variation, but

[8] *Ibid., Lietuvos Uzsienio Prekyba* (Foreign Trade of Lithuania), Kaunas, volumes for 1929, 1932, 1925, and 1938.

failed to reveal any decided tendency toward increase or decrease.

Credit for the increase of exports of food products belongs

TABLE 41

SHIFTING OF COMMODITY GROUPS IN IMPORTS 1925–39

(*Percent*)

YEAR	LIVESTOCK	FOOD PRODUCTS	RAW AND SEMIFINISHED PRODUCTS	FINISHED GOODS	GOLD AND SILVER
1925	0.47	24.44	20.85	53.29	0.95
1926	0.04	18.61	26.88	54.25	1.19
1927	0.05	18.43	26.97	54.52	0.03
1928	0.03	17.43	26.86	55.59	0.09
1929	0.03	18.17	27.71	54.01	0.08
1930	0.09	12.44	26.97	60.48	0.02
1931	0.07	10.03	25.92	63.88	0.10
1932	0.02	10.27	29.41	60.03	0.27
1933	0.04	7.59	34.62	57.30	0.45
1934	0.03	8.02	35.25	56.27	0.43
1935	0.02	6.29	35.64	56.62	1.43
1936	0.05	5.98	36.15	56.63	1.19
1937	0.10	4.89	38.32	56.53	0.16
1938	0.02	5.04	35.21	59.49	0.24
1939	0.01	4.75	35.91	59.82	0.21

to the Central Union of Dairy Coöperative Societies, Pienocentras, in the field of milk products, and to the Maistas Corporation in the field of meat products.

In the exports of Lithuania the commodity items involved are not as varied as they are in the imports. The foreign trade statistics of Lithuania for 1938 show that 1,125 separate items of goods were involved in imports while the export list contained only 500 separate items.

Livestock is not of much importance in the list of imports; the volume is small, livestock being imported only for the purpose of improving Lithuania's breeding stock.

The food products group comprises, among other commodities, salted herring, rice, fruits, coffee, sugar, and salt. Within the period 1924–31 the most significant item of import in the food products group was sugar, which in 1924 amounted to 14.4 million litas. In the same year salted herring accounted for 5.7 million litas; fruits, 2.2 million litas; salt, 2.2 million litas; rice, 1.5 million litas; and coffee, 0.6 million litas. The imports in this group increased further, and in 1927 sugar accounted for 20.5 million litas; salted herring, 9.1 million litas; salt, 2.8 million litas; fruits, 2.1 million litas; rice, 1.8 million litas; and coffee, 1.0 million litas. In later years the value of these staples decreased, so that in 1936 herring amounted to only 3.3 million litas and in 1938, 3.9 million litas. The greatest decrease was in sugar imports, which in 1930 accounted for 31.7 million litas; in 1937, 0.14 million litas; and in 1938, 0.2 million litas. For the decrease in sugar imports credit is given to the local sugar refineries and to the development of domestic sugar-beet growing. The decrease in sugar imports affected the food products group imports so that its percentage value in the total imports decreased from 24.44 in 1926 to 4.75 in 1939. Salt imports do not show any major change; in 1936 such imports accounted for 1.7 million litas and in 1938 for 1.6 million litas.[4] The same may be said of the other merchandise in this group.

In the group of raw and semimanufactured products the most significant import items are fertilizers, metals, liquid

[4] C.S.B., *Lietuvos Uzsienio Prekyba 1929* (The Foreign Trade of Lithuania in 1929) and volumes for 1933–1938.

fuels, petroleum products, coal, cement, and tobacco. In 1924 the imports of fertilizers accounted for 6.0 million litas; metals, 5.1; coal, 9.5; liquid fuel, 4.4; cement, 1.9; and tobacco, 1.5. Some of these items doubled in imports a few years later. In 1928 fertilizer imports accounted for 13.2 million litas; metals, 10.7; coal, 11.3; liquid fuel, 9.6; cement, 4.7; and tobacco, 3.2. In 1938 the imports were: fertilizer, 10.89 million litas; metals, 17.73; coal, 11.01; liquid fuel, 7.35; cement, 6.26; and tobacco, 1.65. Most of these items are very important necessities and cannot be replaced by substitutes or otherwise supplied. That is why the imports in this group increased from 20.85 percent of total import value in 1925 to 35.21 percent in 1939.

Of manufactured goods imported by Lithuania, the most important are chemical products, textile goods, machinery, metal goods, automobiles, motorcycles, rubber products, and various types of apparatus. This group accounted for 53.29 percent of the total value of imports in 1925 and increased to 59.82 percent in 1939. This type of merchandise undoubtedly will retain its important position in the nation's foreign trade.

LITHUANIA'S FOREIGN TRADE ACCORDING TO COUNTRY

Germany and Great Britain in 1938 accounted for 66.18 percent of the exports and 53.30 percent of the imports of Lithuania. Important also in the foreign trade of Lithuania were Soviet Russia, Belgium, Czechoslovakia, Holland, France, Switzerland, Denmark, Sweden, Latvia, and the United States of America. These countries, together with the United Kingdom and Germany, in 1938 accounted for 95.19 percent of the total value of Lithuania's exports and 89.09 percent of her imports.

Table 42

THE DISTRIBUTION OF LITHUANIA'S FOREIGN TRADE WITH RESPECT TO COUNTRIES 1925–38

(In Millions of Litas)

YEAR	UNITED KINGDOM		GERMANY		SOVIET RUSSIA		BELGIUM		CZECHOSLOVAKIA		HOLLAND		U.S.A.	
	Exp.	*Imp.*	*Exp.*	*Imp.*	*Exp.*	*Imp.*	*Exp.*	*Imp.*	*Exp.*	*Imp.*	*Exp.*	*Imp.*	*Exp.*	*Imp.*
1925	58.6	20.9	123.2	143.0	6.4	4.1	2.5	2.5	2.4	13.8	5.6	4.8	3.6	18.3
1926	63.1	19.1	118.6	129.5	2.1	3.2	7.2	2.6	10.1	15.1	2.4	8.3	2.1	10.7
1927	61.1	17.9	126.8	141.2	1.1	6.4	4.9	3.2	3.8	13.9	4.3	9.1	4.4	14.5
1928	52.3	19.3	148.3	146.8	3.7	9.1	4.3	3.7	0.8	13.1	5.4	9.2	2.4	20.5
1929	57.4	26.0	195.9	150.2	1.3	13.1	4.3	5.3	0.9	19.3	10.7	10.0	4.4	16.7
1930	65.0	24.1	199.9	151.4	5.2	13.8	6.8	7.4	0.4	18.0	6.8	10.0	2.6	14.7
1931	90.4	19.7	125.4	130.7	8.3	17.2	10.7	7.9	0.2	19.6	4.9	7.3	2.0	11.0
1932	78.3	18.0	74.0	67.2	6.7	10.2	3.4	7.6	0.2	12.6	3.9	4.5	1.0	6.3
1933	71.6	24.3	52.5	51.0	2.7	7.8	4.5	7.5	1.3	8.6	3.8	4.7	5.3	4.2
1934	62.7	35.1	31.8	38.8	7.5	6.0	6.4	7.9	4.4	9.1	4.6	5.0	4.8	4.0
1935	69.5	47.9	5.4	14.7	13.1	13.6	11.9	4.9	5.6	9.2	8.0	6.0	3.0	3.8
1936	92.2	57.0	20.6	14.4	10.1	14.7	10.5	13.7	7.1	7.5	5.5	7.1	6.7	4.4
1937	96.6	59.3	34.5	46.4	11.1	17.9	7.8	16.7	7.0	6.9	9.5	8.9	6.8	7.4
1938	91.8	69.2	62.5	54.7	13.3	15.0	10.7	8.6	9.6	8.5	8.1	10.7	5.6	8.2

TRADE WITH THE UNITED KINGDOM

Although the turnover in goods between Lithuania and the United Kingdom is not inconsiderable, comparatively speaking, there is no commercial treaty, as such, existing between the two countries. In lieu of a treaty there is an understanding arrived at through an exchange of notes in 1922 between the legation of the United Kingdom in Riga and the Ministry of Foreign Affairs of Lithuania. According to this arrangement each country enjoys the privileges provided by the most-favored-nation clause.[5] Of the exports of Lithuania, the United Kingdom was the second importer in 1925, having absorbed 24.15 percent of the total exports. This percentage decreased to 17.41 in 1929 and then rose to 48.38 in 1936. In 1938, 39.38 percent of Lithuania's exports went to the United Kingdom. In so far as imports are concerned, the United Kingdom does not enjoy as high a percentage as in the exports of Lithuania. For example, in 1925 the imports from Great Britain accounted for only 8.28 percent; they fell to 6.75 percent in 1928 and then rose to 37.28 percent in 1935. In 1938 the imports from the United Kingdom accounted for 30.93 percent. As stated above and as may be seen from Table 42, Lithuania's trade with the United Kingdom, having been in second place in 1925, advanced to first place in 1932 and held this position up to the outbreak of the war of 1939. The chief goods involved in the trade with the United Kingdom in recent years are listed in Table 43.

Forest products, raw wool, and cotton fabrics were the only items in the exchange of goods between Lithuania and the United Kingdom that did not show an increase in the period 1935–38.

[5] *V.Z. Nr. 231, eil. 1497.*

TABLE 43

COMMODITIES INVOLVED IN THE TRADE WITH GREAT BRITAIN 1935–38

(*In Thousands of Litas*)

A. EXPORTS	1935	1936	1937	1938
Total exports	69,514	92,153	96,581	91,824
Bacon	17,405	22,584	22,828	24,051
Butter	18,302	25,541	27,944	31,831
Eggs	1,387	3,660	3,914	4,647
Boards and planks	6,581	5,622	9,145	5,260
Woodpulp	4,570	4,908	4,867	4,329
Veneer	3,638	3,479	3,608	1,610
Flax and tow	5,177	12,434	12,921	12,524
B. IMPORTS				
Herring	2,148	3,224	2,345	3,541
Superphosphates	1,238	1,078	1,130	1,745
Sheet iron	900	1,398	1,506	2,042
Coal	5,252	6,178	7,686	8,452
Cement	1,430	1,512	2,141	4,748
Raw wool	1,633	1,675	2,177	1,524
Woolen yarn	3,648	6,406	6,753	7,534
Cotton yarn	5,210	6,208	5,943	5,306
Woolen fabrics	3,312	4,283	4,400	4,139
Cotton fabrics (raw and bleached)	1,125	1,300	1,325	1,006
Dyed cotton fabrics	3,971	6,406	4,890	3,906

TRADE WITH GERMANY

The trade treaty between Lithuania and Germany was concluded June 1, 1923, ratified July 31, 1924, and put in force May 5, 1926. This treaty expired February 22, 1929.[6]

[6] *V.Z. Nr. 173, eil. 1196.*

From the first years of Lithuania's independence, the dominating country in her foreign trade was Germany, but proper statistics up to 1925 are lacking. In 1925, 50.74 percent of Lithuania's exports went to Germany, while imports from Germany constituted 56.61 percent of Lithuania's total imports. In 1929 the exports to Germany rose to 59.40 percent, while at the same time exports to the United Kingdom fell to 17.41 percent.

The sharp decrease in Germany's share in the foreign trade of Lithuania, caused partly by the introduction in Germany of agrarian protectionist restrictions and partly by misunderstandings of a noneconomic character (the Klaipeda controversy) started in 1932,[7] when Germany tried to obtain political concessions through exerting economic pressure.

The lowest ebb was reached in 1935, with the exports accounting for 3.57 percent and imports for 11.40 percent. In 1936 a new trade treaty was concluded between Lithuania and Germany,[8] after which time the trade between the two countries received a new impetus.

The principal commodities involved in the foreign trade with Germany in recent years are given in Table 44. The total imports from Germany in 1938 amounted to 54,704,000 litas as compared with 46,381,000 litas in 1937 and 14,400,000 litas in 1936. Among the principal commodities imported from Germany in 1938, besides those listed in Table 44, were various fertilizers (3,194,100 litas), cement (968,400 litas), brass products (1,016,600 litas), dynamo machinery (1,228,900 litas), and bicycles (1,619,800 litas).[9]

[7] *Report*, p. 88.
[8] *V.Z., Nr. 552, eil. 3839.*
[9] *L.U. Prekyba 1938*, pp. 567–613.

TABLE 44

COMMODITIES INVOLVED IN THE TRADE WITH GERMANY 1935–38

(In Thousands of Litas)

A. EXPORTS	1935	1936	1937	1938
Total exports	5,435	20,599	34,479	62,493
Live pigs	2	4,046	7,504	10,079
Live poultry	0.6	1,492	1,535	2,282
Beef	3	247	1,169	2,266
Slaughtered poultry and game	670	1,003	1,130	1,319
Butter	63	2,928	7,589	11,146
Eggs	4	542	1,532	2,304
Boards and planks	356	2,291	1,886	2,053
Flax and tow	35	1,384	923	5,893
B. IMPORTS				
Iron rails	—	4	1,661	62
Woolen fabrics	36	112	1,007	617
Cotton fabrics (dyed)	81	128	937	878
Factory machinery	331	316	1,714	1,740
Machine parts	516	502	1,232	1,857
Motor cars	16	122	1,137	1,233
Chassis	50	187	1,196	1,566
Scientific apparatus and instruments	239.5	359	981	1,145

TRADE WITH SOVIET RUSSIA

Although Soviet Russia is close to Lithuania, the exchange of goods between these two countries, up to the war of 1939, was comparatively small. The exports to Soviet Russia, which in 1925 accounted for 2.66 percent of Lithuania's total, in 1929 fell to 0.39 percent. From 1930 the volume of exports to Soviet Russia increased, reaching 8.59 percent in 1935, which ranked her third among countries importing from Lithuania. This place she retained until 1938, in which year exports to Soviet Russia amounted to 13,337,800 litas or 5.72 percent. The number of items exported to Soviet Russia was small, and of these the principal commodities were pigs and hides.

TABLE 45

COMMODITIES INVOLVED IN THE TRADE WITH SOVIET RUSSIA 1936–38

(In Thousands of Litas)

A. EXPORTS	1936	1937	1938
Total exports	10,087	11,056	13,338
Live pigs over 99 pounds (45 kgm)	7,092	8,645	10,908
Hides for soles	—	1,111	1,390
Calfskins	129	952	650
B. IMPORTS			
Total imports	14,737	17,896	14,954
Salt	1,134	1,048	1,039
Fertilizers	946	1,094	1,487
Lumber	3,017	3,359	2,032
Liquid fuel	3,149	2,936	3,236
Coal	1,231	1,619	1,407
Dyed cotton fabrics	887	958	973

In imports Soviet Russia held a somewhat better position. Thus, imports from Soviet Russia in 1925 accounted for 1.63 percent; in 1929 they rose to 4.28 percent and in 1935 to 10.55 percent. In 1938 the imports from Soviet Russia amounted to 14,954,400 litas, or 6.69 percent of the total imports of Lithuania.

According to the arrangement of September 24, 1928, concluded through an exchange of notes, each of these countries enjoyed the most-favored-nation treatment.[10] On August 29, 1931, a protocol was signed and notes were exchanged regarding the legal status of the commercial representatives of Soviet Russia in Lithuania and on the reciprocal transit communication. Before the occupation in 1940, Soviet Russia looked upon Lithuania, as well as upon the other Baltic states, as an area of competition between German and English capital.[11] After the outbreak of war in 1939, Soviet Russia apparently became interested in the competition between German and English capital, and stepped in as a third rival in preparation to occupy Lithuania. This was evident particularly from the fact that the Mutual Assistance Treaty of October 10, 1939, was followed by a commercial treaty, signed on October 16, 1939, according to which the turnover of goods between Lithuania and Soviet Russia was to be increased to 40 million litas. Conditions for the increase of trade with Soviet Russia seemed favorable, because of the Allied blockade of Germany and the latter's counterblockade, which, of course, jeopardized the trade between Lithuania and the Allies.

TRADE WITH BELGIUM

Trade with Belgium was regulated according to the Provisional Commercial Agreement of August 16, 1928. Belgium's share of Lithuania's exports, 1.01 percent in 1925, rose to 2.82 percent in 1928. Later the trade with Belgium

[10] *V.Z. Nr. 285, eil. 1848.*

[11] Nauchno-Issledovatelskii Institut Monopolii Vneshnei Torgovli, *Torgovie Otnoshenia SSSR s Kapitalisticheskimi Stranami* (Trade Relations of U.S.S.R. with Capitalistic Countries), Moskva, 1938, p. 241.

increased to such an extent that in 1935 she took 7.82 percent of Lithuania's total exports and was the source of 3.84 percent of Lithuania's imports. In 1938 Belgium accounted for 4.58 percent of exports and 3.86 percent of imports. In 1938 the total exports to Belgium amounted to 10,675,700 litas, with rye, barley, oats, and vetch accounting for 6,179,-500 litas. Imports from Belgium in 1938 amounted to 8,630,-400 litas as against 16,749,600 litas in 1937. In the long list of goods imported, the largest item is pig iron, which in 1938 accounted for 4,056,600 litas as against 6,626,900 litas in 1937.

TRADE WITH LATVIA

Trade with Latvia is regulated by the Commercial Treaty of April 10, 1935, and the Clearing Agreement of the same date.[12] The latter was amended by the arrangement of November 30, 1936, and ratified on December 14, 1936.[13]

In 1925 Latvia held third place in the exports of Lithuania, in that year accounting for 8.53 percent, and in the following year 10.46 percent. In later years Latvia's share in the trade of Lithuania had decreased until in 1938 it was only 1.17 percent of exports and 1.10 percent of imports. The leading item in exports to Latvia for several years was horses, in 1936 valued at 1,591,000 litas; in 1937, 706,900 litas; and in 1938, 1,208,100 litas.

The more important import items from Latvia were radios, accounting for 125,800 litas in 1938 as against 188,000 litas in 1937; bicycles, 169,400 litas in 1938; glass, 283,100 litas in 1938; and several kinds of machinery.

[12] *V.Z. Nr. 481.*
[13] *V.Z. Nr. 562.*

TRADE WITH THE UNITED STATES OF AMERICA

Trade with the United States was regulated by a special arrangement through "Exchange of notes between the United States of America and the Republic of Lithuania, embody-

TABLE 46

COMMODITIES INVOLVED IN THE TRADE WITH THE UNITED STATES 1936–38

(In Thousands of Litas)

A. EXPORTS	1936	1937	1938
Total exports	6,696	6,848	5,624
Meat	1,755	1,993	2,498
Woodpulp	2,800	4,019	2,792
B. IMPORTS			
Total imports	4,386	7,383	8,236
Tobacco	491	392	297
Oil	357	567	767
Raw cotton	494	615	572
Automobile tires and tubes	98	158	254
Cotton fabrics (dyed)	57	553	288
Automobiles	108	707	1,058

ing a commercial agreement between these States" [14] of December 23, 1925, ratified on March 24, 1926.[15] According to this arrangement, each party enjoys "unconditional most-

[14] Pranas Dailide, *Lietuvos sutartys su svetimomis valstybemis. Tomas I. 1919–1929.* (Collection of Treaties Concluded between Lithuania and Foreign States, Vol. I, 1919–1929), Kaunas, 1930, pp. 414–18.
[15] *V.Z. Nr. 231, eil. 1496.*

favored-nation treatment." Trade relations with the United States were begun in the early years of independent Lithuania. As far back as 1925 the imports of Lithuania from the United States amounted to 18,310,800 litas, or 7.25 percent, while the exports to the United States were only a fraction of this sum, namely 3,593,800 litas, or 1.48 percent. The percentage of exports to the United States in recent years increased somewhat, while that of imports decreased. Thus in 1936 the United States took 3.24 percent of the exports of Lithuania and sent 2.85 percent of the imports. In 1938 the exports of the United States to Lithuania amounted to 5,624,100 litas, or 2.41 percent, while the imports totaled 8,236,400 litas, or 3.68 percent.

Among the other countries trading with Lithuania the most noteworthy were: Czechoslovakia, which in 1938 received 4.13 percent of exports and 3.79 percent of imports; Holland, which in the same years sent 3.47 percent of imports and took 4.76 percent in exports; France, with 2.49 percent of imports and 3.17 percent of exports; and Switzerland, 2.20 percent of imports and 2.84 percent of exports.

Chapter V

THE FINANCE OF LITHUANIA

The financial aspect of Lithuania's reconstruction after 1918 involves a discussion of her currency, her state finance, and her public debt.

CURRENCY

Up to the time of the World War of 1914–18, Russian ruble notes circulated in Lithuania. As early as 1915, when the first German troops entered Lithuania, a decree was proclaimed which made German marks equally acceptable with the Russian rubles. (Exchange rate: 2.16 marks for 1 gold ruble.) [1]

On April 17, 1915, by special decree, an institution under the name Darlehnkasse Ost (Loan Bank of the East) was created and made a special department of Ostbank für Handel und Gewerbe. The main function of this bank was to issue *Obost* rubles [2] and to serve as a state bank in the occupied region. The official exchange rate of the *Obost* rubles issued by the Darlehnkasse Ost was as follows: one *Obost* ruble equaled one Russian ruble or two German (or *Obost*) marks. By a decree of August 6, 1916, the German administration promised to redeem *Obost* rubles with genuine

[1] *Lietuvos Bankas, First Decade, 1922–1932,* Kaunas, 1932, p. 2.

[2] One *Obost* ruble equaled two *Obost* marks, one bank note having both inscriptions.

Russian rubles put into circulation by Darlehnkasse Ost. But on March 30, 1917, this promise was retracted and redemption by German marks was promised at the rate of two marks for one ruble.[3]

After the declaration of independence, February 16, 1918, because of unsettled conditions Lithuania was unable quickly to introduce her own bank notes. The Provisional Government signed with the Darlehnkasse Ost an agreement by which the notes were to remain in circulation until a Lithuanian bank of issue could be organized. The sums in circulation at that time, as estimated by Professor Rimka, are shown in Table 47.

TABLE 47

GERMAN OBOST NOTES IN CIRCULATION 1917–22

YEAR	NOTES IN CIRCULATION	VALUE IN LITAS [a]
	(Millions of Obost marks)	*(Millions)*
1917	125.75	186.77
1918 (March 31)	165.65	327.30
1918 (Dec. 31)	290.90	363.62
1920 (July)	546.80	138.50
1921 (July)	779.80	101.70
1922 (July)	2,000.00	63.00
1922 (Sept.)	3,500.00	17.00

[a] One litas equals 0.150462 grams fine gold.

It may be observed that the number of notes in circulation increased very rapidly while their value in litas decreased. In September, 1922, the total of notes in circulation was more than ten times greater than on December 31, 1918, while at the same time their value in litas was only one

[3] *Ibid.*

twenty-first as great. In January, 1919, the rate of exchange was 8.27 marks to the dollar, while one year later, in February, 1920, it was 98.994 marks, and in the beginning of 1922, 200 marks. On October 1, 1922, the day redemption of the *Obost* marks commenced, one dollar equaled 1,650 marks; on October 2, 1,815 marks. Russian rubles were redeemed on October 1, 1922, at 0.004 litas.[4]

A special law for the establishment of Lietuvos Bankas (the Bank of Lithuania) was passed on August 11, 1922.[5] The financial basis of the bank is 12,000,000 litas capital stock consisting of 120,000 shares of 100 litas par value each. Although Lietuvos Bankas, before Soviet occupation, was a private enterprise in its organization, it was under government control and the general director was appointed by the president of the republic upon recommendation of the Council of Ministers. The Law of Establishment of the Lietuvos Bankas grants a special concession to permit the issuance of notes for twenty years, which period may be prolonged by law.

With the first issue of litas notes on October 1, 1922, the redemption of the *Obost* marks at the market exchange rate was begun. The Russian rubles at that time were almost worthless, and the value of *Obost* marks was just a fraction of the original value. This caused a great loss to the population of Lithuania, wiping out everybody's savings and creating generally chaotic credit conditions. There is no question but that Germany was responsible for the inflation and loss in the value of *Obost* marks and that Lithuania had the right to demand reparations. Negotiations for that purpose were

[4] Kazys Sruoga, *Die Wirtschaft der Republik Litauen und ihre Notenemission*, Kaunas, 1930, pp. 15–18.

[5] *Lietuvos Bankas, First Decade, 1922–1932,* Kaunas, 1932, pp. 10–14; *V.Z. Nr. 199, par. 1347.*

started in March, 1922, in Kaunas. Reparation was sought for the compulsory introduction of *Obost* marks and the use of issuance rights from August, 1916, until November, 1919, when the German army finally withdrew. The loss to Lithuania was estimated at 5,383 million marks, which sum was demanded by the Lithuanian delegation. Due to the fact that the Germans refused to recognize these demands, negotiations were discontinued. They were resumed in Berlin in May, 1923.[6] These negotiations resulted in a treaty concluded on May 31, 1923, of which the first paragraph says: "Both contracting parties agree not to raise any claims against each other, originating from events of the World War."[7]

After three months of operation of Lietuvos Bankas—that is, on December 31, 1922—there were 30.38 million litas in circulation. The coverage in gold of the notes in circulation accounted for 50 percent and that in gold and foreign exchange for 109.1 percent. The amount of litas in circulation grew, while the coverage in gold decreased somewhat, but it was never less than the one-third prescribed by law. Thus on December 31, 1923, there were 60.07 million litas in circulation; in 1924, 92.98; in 1925, 81.92; in 1926, 86.79; and in 1927, 96.61.[8]

The issue activities of Lietuvos Bankas in later years are indicated by Table 48. At the end of 1938 the notes in circulation amounted to 141.70 million litas, exceeding the previous all-time high of 1930, while in April, 1939, it reached 181.65 millions, a new all-time peak. The coverage in gold

[6] A. Moravskis, *Lietuvos Finansai, Pinigai, kreditas ir bankai* Lietuvoje pries kara ir dabar, II dalis. (The Finance of Lithuania: Money, Credit and Banking in Lithuania before the War and at Present. Part II), Kaunas, 1925, pp. 33–35.

[7] Dailide, *op. cit.*, p. 199; *V.Z. Nr. 173, par. 1197.*

[8] *Lietuvos Bankas Bulletin,* Feb. 19, 1932, p. 18.

TABLE 48

THE ISSUE ACTIVITIES OF LIETUVOS BANKAS
1928–39

YEAR ENDING DEC. 31	BANK NOTES IN CIRCULATION (*Million litas*)	GOLD RESERVE (*Million litas*)	FOREIGN BILLS (*Million litas*)	PERCENTAGE OF COVERAGE IN GOLD AND FOREIGN BILLS
1928	84.77	34.27	43.62	91.9
1929	94.83	35.08	78.48	119.8
1930	117.16	39.39	86.32	107.3
1931	108.95	50.14	33.17	76.5
1932	96.21	49.07	15.96	67.6
1933	89.92	52.00	15.34	76.8
1934	88.24	52.14	8.38	68.6
1935	103.50	36.14	9.91	44.5
1936	110.35	73.10	4.08	69.9
1937	116.56	79.04	1.87	69.4
1938	141.70	64.75	4.83	49.1
1939	165.93	57.71	2.50	37.1

and foreign bills was comparatively high, being 49.1 percent.

The highest number of notes in circulation and the lowest coverage were reached in November, 1939. This situation was largely due to the disturbed economic conditions in Lithuania in that year. It will be recalled that in March, 1939, Lithuania was forced to give up her only port, Klaipeda. This transaction was executed in great haste, under the pressure of the German war machine, as a result of which it became necessary to support and furnish with food, shelter, and work about 15,000 refugees.

A few months later over 100,000 refugees from Poland poured into Lithuania, as a result of the war between Germany and Poland. Undoubtedly this circumstance caused a great drain on gold and foreign exchange reserves.

The litas was never devalued, and it held its original gold parity until Soviet occupation on June 15, 1940. Shortly after occupation the financial structure of Lithuania was destroyed entirely. The litas was substituted by the ruble. All savings accounts over 1,000 litas (approximately $165.00) were confiscated. Though the purchasing value of the Soviet ruble was much less than that of the litas, nevertheless the litas officially was rated at 90 kopeks (a kopek equals one-hundredth of a ruble). The Germans who replaced the Russians set the official exchange rate at 50 pfennigs, or half a German mark, to a ruble.

STATE FINANCE

The state finance and the economic policy of the republic of Lithuania were guided by the minister of finance. In 1923, the first year for which statistics are available, the revenue amounted to 166.30 million litas against expenditures of 166 million litas.[9] The following year's revenue increased to 235.79 million litas and expenditures to 232.32, leaving a favorable balance of 3.47 million litas. The highest balance was gained in 1929 when the revenues of 293.79 million litas exceeded expenditures by 26.10 million litas. But in 1931 and 1932 expenditures exceeded revenue. In 1931 the total income amounted to 315.09 million litas, expenditures were 335.30 million litas, and the deficit was thus 20.21 million litas. In 1932 the deficit was somewhat smaller: 12.40 million litas. The budget of 1938 was practically balanced, the revenue amounting to 366.48 million litas, while the expenditures totaled 366.49 million litas. In 1939 revenues amounted to 361.78 and expenditures to 356.54 million litas. The growth of the budget during the years of independence was

[9] C.S.B., volume for 1927.

considerable, the 1938 figures being more than double those of 1923.[10]

The greater part of government income is received from indirect taxes, comprising excises, state monopolies, and customs duties. This group in 1936 yielded 22.59 percent of the total revenue; in 1937, 25.74 percent; and in 1938, 24.24 percent. Next in importance is the yield of government enterprises, comprising the revenue from post, telegraph, telephone, railways, and mixed enterprises in which the government has interest. Revenue from this group in 1936 accounted for 16.04 percent; in 1937, 15.60 percent; and in 1938, 14.76 percent. The third source of income according to percentage of the total revenue, is direct taxation, which in 1938 accounted for 14.38 percent.

In expenditures, the highest percentage goes to the Ministry of Defence, which in 1938 accounted for 23.24 percent of the total expenses. Second place falls to the Ministry of Communication, which in 1938 used 19.79 percent of total expenditures. Third place is held by the Ministry of Education, with 16.01 percent. Then follow the Ministry of Agriculture with 13.86 percent, the Ministry of Finance with 11.30 percent, and the Ministry of Interior with 8.70 percent.[11]

PUBLIC DEBT

The public debt of Lithuania is comparatively small; it is less than that of either of the other Baltic states, amounting at the end of 1937 to 47 litas per capita, while Latvia's was 80 litas and Estonia's 180 litas per capita.[12]

The debts of Lithuania may be divided into two groups:

[10] *Lietuvos Banko Biuletenis No. 46,* Kaunas, 1939, p. 8.
[11] C.S.B., 1938, pp. 315–19.
[12] Report of C.C.I.C., *Ten Years of Lithuanian Economy,* 1938, p. 146.

(1) debts which originated in the period 1918–22 during the struggle for reëstablishment of the nation's independence and (2) subsequent debts contracted for reconstruction purposes. The debt to the United States for various medicaments, clothing, and foodstuffs obtained from the American military camps in France and from the American Relief Administration belongs in the first group. According to the agreement of September 22, 1924, with the United States, the principal was $4,981,628.03 and accrued interest of 4¼ percent from June 30, 1919, until June 15, 1924, amounted to $1,049,918.94, so that the total debt was $6,031,546.97. Of this amount, $1,546.97 was paid on September 22, 1924, and the remainder, $6,030,000, was to be funded into bonds bearing 3 percent interest until June 15, 1934, and 3⅓ percent after that date until the whole sum was paid. The principal was to be paid in the course of 62 years in fixed amounts each year. Thus, the first amount, $30,000, was due on June 15, 1925, and the last, $227,000, was to fall due on June 15, 1986.[13]

According to the estimate of Moulton,[14] Lithuania, up to June 30, 1931, had paid $1,128,600. The latest payments made by Lithuania to the United States were token payments in the sums of $10,000 on June 15, and $7,000 on December 15, 1933, but after the passage of the Johnson Act Lithuania made no further payments. On May 5, 1934, Attorney General Cummings of the United States pointed out that Lithuania was one among the six foreign governments[15] indebted to the United States government which was not in default under the terms of the Johnson Act, because she

[13] Dailide, *op. cit.*, p. 310.

[14] Harold G. Moulton and Leo Pasvolsky, *War Debts and World Prosperity*, Washington, D.C., 1932, p. 293.

[15] Finland, Great Britain, Czechoslovakia, Italy, Latvia, and Lithuania.

had made token payments as evidence of good faith in connection with her debt installments.[16]

According to later interpretations of the Johnson Act, however, the State Department on May 10, 1934, informed European debtor governments that while token payments

TABLE 49

FOREIGN AND DOMESTIC DEBTS OF LITHUANIA AT THE END OF 1939

	LITAS
A. FOREIGN DEBTS	
Debts to the U.S.A.	38,661,000 [a]
Debts to Great Britain	718,200 [b]
Liberty Loan	2,939,700
Match Monopoly Loan	25,193,500 [c]
Debts for public works	359,500
Short-term loans	1,043,400
TOTAL	68,915,300
B. DOMESTIC DEBTS	
4½% Domestic Loan of 1935	12,260,400
4½% Domestic Loan of 1936	11,893,600
Treasury Bills of 1937	2,138,300
4½% Domestic Loan of 1939	4,439,000
Vilnius Loan of 1939	15,420,500
Debentures of war collections	16,400
Debts for public works	4,063,000
TOTAL	65,231,200
TOTAL PUBLIC DEBT	134,146,500

[a] Total debts to the United States: 41,600,700 litas or $6,864,801.
[b] Total debts to Great Britain: 1,456,700 litas or £50,849.
[c] $4,157,350.

[16] *New York Times,* May 6, 1934.

would be acceptable on June 15 when the following installments on the war debts were to have been due, such payments would not serve to free them of being considered in default within the meaning of the Johnson Act.[17] Pressed by adverse economic conditions prevailing in that year, Lithuania was unable to meet her obligation and thus was classified "in default." It must be remembered, however, that exports of Lithuania in that year were the smallest since 1923 and the economic depression in general was at its worst.

Another sum in this group is the debt of 1920 to Great Britain for war material deliveries to the amount of 7,300,000 litas (£150,000). The total debts originating in the period of the struggle for independence amount to 50,700,000 litas.

In the group of debts for reconstruction the greatest item is the Match Monopoly Loan of $4,500,000, which was contracted in 1930 in Sweden for the transfer of the match monopoly to the Swedish Match Manufacturing Company.

[17] *New York Times,* May 11, 1934.

Chapter VI

SUMMARY AND CONCLUSIONS

From the facts and figures cited in the preceding pages we see that in the short period of twenty-two years of independence since the World War little Lithuania has lacked neither initiative nor industry. Surveying the devastation left behind by the three neighboring armies which had overrun the country at various periods of the war, Lithuania gathered her tiny forces and resolutely set about the gigantic task of reconstruction. Perhaps it was this grim determination and buoyant enthusiasm in their regained freedom that gave this new republic the necessary momentum. Perhaps it was the inspiration of the glorious days of Vytautas when Lithuania was a world power combined with the well-known native trait of dogged perseverance that enabled this ancient Baltic people to turn from problem to problem with boundless vigor.

That an objective résumé of her efforts and accomplishments does not find the country wanting in creditable results may be seen by even a cursory glance at almost any one of the tables in this book. To compare the Lithuania of 1939 with the Lithuania of the early post-war years is to acknowledge that great strides were made in her agriculture through the well-planned land reform, the development of coöperatives, and the improvement of livestock husbandry and dairying. Furthermore, her war-torn industry has been reconstructed to suit her own particular needs.

Her foreign trade has been showing almost continuous expansion. Her increased production, as well as consuming power, bespeak an attendant higher standard of living. All these facts certainly justify Lithuania's participation in the family of nations and her existence as a separate independent economic entity.

The future course of Lithuania's economic development cannot be predicted because of the series of political crises of 1939, 1940, and 1941. On March 22, 1939, Lithuania was forced to agree to the cession of Klaipeda to Germany. Though Lithuania was given a so-called "free zone," the effect was as of being forced to gasp for air with someone else's lungs. Through this cession Lithuania not only lost 703,741 acres of territory (5.1 percent of her total area) but was deprived of 13 percent of her industry, with 26 percent of her wage earners. The total industrial production of Klaipeda territory in 1937 amounted to 116 million litas, or 30.7 percent of Lithuania's total production.

Before Lithuania had time to adjust her national economy to the new conditions, the war broke out between Germany on the one side and Poland and the Allies on the other. This upset the normal economic life even more. The immediate result of the war was the partition of Poland between Germany and, as a silent partner, Soviet Russia. This was soon followed by the signing of mutual assistance pacts between Soviet Russia on the one side and Estonia, Latvia, and Lithuania on the other. Baltic states actually had no other choice than to sign on the dotted line.

Lithuania signed her pact on October 10, 1939, thereby regaining Vilnius, with 2,569 square miles of territory and about 457,500 inhabitants, although according to the Peace Treaty between Lithuania and Soviet Russia of July 12, 1920, Lithuania should have regained 12,448 square miles. Lithuania's industry was partly compensated for the loss of Klaipeda. But the industry in the Vilnius territory is not nearly as developed as that in the Klaipeda region. According to the approximate statistics there are in that part of the Vilnius territory which was returned to Lithuania 159 industrial establishments with 5,900 employees. Also, the agricultural standard in this region is substantially below that in other sections of Lithuania. As a step toward improving agricultural and social conditions, the government of Lithuania was about to put into effect its land reform act of 1922, but the Soviet occupation in June, 1940, interrupted this work.

The next blow to the country's fortunes came as a result of the sudden outbreak of war between Germany and Soviet Russia on June 22, 1941. On the following day, Lithuanian patriots arose in rebellion against Bolshevik terrorism and the institution of mass deportations of Lithuanians to Siberia; they were successful enough to drive the Bolsheviks from Kaunas, Vilnius, and other Lithuanian cities. The Lithuanians set up at once a provisional government. But soon the Germans, in pursuit of the retreating Red Army, overran all of Lithuania, dissolved the Lithuanian government, and by autocratic decrees began to shape their economy more to the Nazi-prescribed pattern of "the new order."

As the year 1941 drew to a close, all freedom of action in Lithuania—political, social, and economic—was still suspended. The nation is fully conscious that her future holds another struggle for independence and for a new reconstruction. Lithuania, like many other small nations throughout the world and in Europe in particular, is waiting anxiously for liberation that she again may live in peace and freedom among the free nations of the world; she is waiting for the complete realization of the ideals expressed in the Roosevelt-Churchill Atlantic Charter.

APPENDICES

Appendix A

THE DECLARATION OF INDEPENDENCE[1]

The Council of Lithuania in its meeting on February 16, 1918, voted unanimously to address the governments of Russia, Germany, and other states with the following declaration:

The Council of Lithuania, sole representative of the Lithuanian people, in conformity with the recognized right to national self-determination, and in accordance with the resolution of the Lithuanian Conference held in Vilnius from September 18 to 23, 1917, hereby proclaims the restitution of the independent State of Lithuania, founded on democratic principles, with Vilnius as its capital, and declares the rupture of all ties which formerly bound this State to other nations.

The Council of Lithuania also declares that the foundation of the Lithuanian State and relations with other countries will be finally normalized by a Seimas (parliament), elected in a democratic way by the people of Lithuania.

The Council of Lithuania in informing [the nations addressed] to this effect kindly requests recognition of the independent State of Lithuania.

Vilnius, February 16, 1918 *Signed:*

L. Banaitis	P. Klimas	K. Saulys
Dr. J. Basanavicius	Donatas Malinauskas	J. Sernas
M. Birziska	Vl. Mironas	A. Smetona
K. Bizauskas	S. Narutavicius	J. Smilgevicius
P. Dovydaitis	Alfonsas Petrulis	J. Staugaitis
S. Kairys	Dr. J. Saulys	A. Stulginskis

J. Vailokaitis J. Vileisis

[1] Author's translation from the original Lithuanian.

Appendix B

EXTRACT FROM THE PEACE TREATY WITH RUSSIA

Lithuania on the one part and Russia on the other being determined to base their future mutual relations on justice and right, which would grant to both countries and their peoples the benefits of earnest and peaceful neighborly relations, have to this end decided to start negotiations and have appointed as their delegates:

For the Democratic Republic of Lithuania:

TOMAS NARUSEVICIUS
PETRAS KLIMAS
SIMONAS ROZENBAUMAS
JUOZAS VAILOKAITIS
VYTAUTAS RACKAUSKAS

And for the Federated States of the Soviet Socialist Republics of Russia:

ADOLF ABRAMOVICH IOFFE
ULIAN USEFOVICH MARCHLEVSKI
LEONID LEONIDOVICH BOBLENSKI

The said delegates, having submitted their credentials to one another and found them in good form and order, have agreed on the following:

ARTICLE I

Pursuant to the declaration made by the Federated States of the Soviet Socialist Republics of Russia to the effect that all peoples have the right to self-determination until they become completely separated from the state of which they are a part, Russia without any prejudice recognizes the self-rule and independence of the State of Lithuania with all the juridical consequences resulting from such recognition and for all time renounces with good will all the sovereignty rights of Russia, which it has had in regard to the Lithuanian nation or territory.

The fact that Lithuania ever was under Russian sovereignty does not place the Lithuanian people and the nation or territory under any obligations to Russia.

NOTE: This treaty, consisting of nineteen paragraphs, was signed in Moscow on July 12, 1920, and ratified on August 6, 1920, and it became effective on October 14, 1920.

Appendix C

LITHUANIAN-POLISH PACT

Agreement between Lithuania and Poland with Regard to the Establishment of a Provisional Modus Vivendi Pending a Definite Settlement of Relations between the Two States, Signed at Suvalkai, October 7, 1920 [1]

The Delegation of the Government of Lithuania, composed of:

(1) Representatives of the Lithuanian High Command, Lieutenant General Maksimas Katche, and Commander Aleksandras Sumskis,

(2) Representatives of the Ministry for Foreign Affairs, Messrs. Bronius Balutis, Voldemaras Carneckis, and Mykolas Birziska,

and the Delegation of the Government of Poland, composed of:

(1) Representative of the Polish High Command, Colonel Mieczyslaw Mackiewicz,

(2) Representative of the Ministry for Foreign Affairs, Juljusz Lukasiewicz,

met at the Conference held at Suvalkai from September 30 to October 7, 1920, and, after presenting their credentials, which were found to be in good and due form, concluded the following Agreement:

ARTICLE I: THE LINE OF DEMARCATION

(a) A line of demarcation, which in no way prejudices the territorial claims of the two Contracting Parties, shall be fixed and shall be marked by the following points:

[1] Translation from the Lithuanian by the author.

From the frontier of East Prussia to the confluence of the Juodoji Ancia (Tcharna-Hantcha) with the Nemunas (Niemen) river, i. e., the line fixed by the decision of the Supreme Council on December 8, 1919; thence along the Nemunas river to the mouth of the Grave river; then up the course of the Grave to the point at which it is crossed by the road Merkyne-Ratnycia (Noretch-Rotnitsa); thence in a straight line to the confluence of the Skruoblis with the Merkys river (Meretchanka); thence along the Merkys to the mouth of the Dereznica (Derechnitsa), leaving the village of Salavarciai (Solovertsy) on the Lithuanian side and the village of Male Dubno on the Polish side; thence along the Dereznica (Derechnitsa) to the spot where it is crossed by the Vilnius-Varena (Vilna-Orany) railway, about two kilometers northeast of Varena station; thence along the road through Bartoliai-Kuciai (Bartole-Kucie), Naujadvaris (Nowy-Dvor), Eisiske (Eishishki), Paditve (Podsitwa), Gorodonka, and the station of Bastunai (Bastuny), leaving this road and the Bastunai station in the hands of the Polish authorities.

(b) When hostilities between the Polish and Lithuanian troops have ceased, in conformity with Article 2 of the present Agreement, the line defined above may not under any pretext be crossed by the troops of the two Contracting Parties. Nevertheless, the existence of this line shall not prevent the farmers from cultivating their fields situated on either side of it.

(c) The marking out on the ground of the line of demarcation in those parts of the territory of the former Government of Suvalkai, which are referred to in the decision of the Supreme Council of December 8, 1919, shall be entrusted to the Commission of Control of the League of Nations.

ARTICLE 2: CESSATION OF HOSTILITIES

(a) The two Contracting Parties, confirming and completing the Agreements for the cessation of hostilities between the Polish and Lithuanian armies, which have been accepted during the present Conference, and which have only a provisional character and relate only to certain places, undertake to cease hostilities throughout the entire length of the line of demarcation described in Article 1, paragraph (a) of the present Agreement from the frontier of East Prussia to the meridian of Paturciai (Paturse), about nine kilometers southeast of Eisiske.

(b) After the withdrawal of the Soviet troops to the east of the Vilnius-Lyda railway, military operations between the Polish and Lithuanian troops shall cease on the sector of the line of demarcation between the meridian of the village of Paturciai and the station of Bastunai inclusively.

(c) As regards the cessation of hostilities and the establishment of a line of demarcation between the Lithuanian and Polish troops in the region to the east of the meridian of the station of Bastunai, these questions shall be settled by a special agreement when the Soviet troops have been withdrawn from that region. In case of failure to arrive at such an agreement, the two Contracting Parties reserve the right to appeal to the League of Nations for a solution of these questions.

ARTICLE 3: THE STATION OF VARENA

(a) The Polish authorities undertake to allow Lithuanian trains (except troop trains and trains conveying war material) to pass in either direction between Alytus and Vilnius and to afford to Lithuanian trains at Varena station all assistance and technical facilities for free movement in either direction.

(b) As an exception, the Polish Government consents to allow trains conveying troops and war materials proceeding from Alytus to pass freely through Varena station, provided that the total number of such trains does not exceed seven, that not more than two trains pass in one day, and that they pass through Varena station between seven and seventeen o'clock [Polish time].

(c) The supervision of the execution of the provisions contained in paragraphs (a) and (b) of the present Article shall be entrusted to the Commission of Control of the League of Nations.

ARTICLE 4: EXCHANGE OF PRISONERS

The two Contracting Parties declare that they mutually agree in principle to exchange all prisoners taken by either Contracting Party. The order and date of exchange shall be decided by separate agreement.

ARTICLE 5: DURATION OF AGREEMENT, ETC.

The present Agreement shall come into force at noon on October 10, 1920. This date, however, shall not affect the cessation of hostilities where this has actually taken place. The Agreement shall remain in force until all territorial disputes between Poles and Lithuanians have been finally settled.

In drawing up the present Agreement the two Contracting Parties have used the German General Staff Map, scale 1 : 100,000.

The present Agreement is done in duplicate in the Lithuanian and Polish languages, and signed at Suvalkai, on October 7, 1920.

For the Lithuanian Delegation:

LIEUTENANT GENERAL M. KATCHE
BRONIUS BALUTIS
VOLDEMARAS CARNECKIS
MYKOLAS BIRZISKA
MAJOR ALEKSANDRAS SUMSKIS

For the Polish Delegation:

COLONEL M. MACKIEWICZ
J. LUKASIEWICZ

Appendix D

THE POLISH ULTIMATUM TO LITHUANIA, MARCH, 1939[1]

On the 17th of March, 1938, at 9 P. M. the Lithuanian Minister in Tallinn received through the Polish Minister of that capital the following ultimatum:

By order of my Government I have the honour to communicate to Your Excellency the following:

1. The proposal of the Lithuanian Government of the 14th instant cannot be accepted because it does not give sufficient guarantees regarding security on the frontier, particularly in view of the negative results of all previous attempts at negotiations between Poland and Lithuania.

2. In view of this, the Polish Government declare that they consider that the sole solution which corresponds to the gravity of this situation is that of immediately establishing normal diplomatic relations, without any preliminary conditions whatsoever, this being the only way to regulate questions of neighborly relations of all governments truly animated by the will to avoid incidents dangerous to peace.

3. The Polish Government gives the Lithuanian Government forty-eight hours from the time of the delivery of this note to accept this proposal by communicating that they agree to accredit diplomatic representatives at Kaunas and at Warsaw not later than the 31st of March of this year. Up to that date all conversations of technical or other character between the Polish and Lithuanian Governments must be carried on by their envoys extraordinary and ministers plenipotentiary at Tallinn.

[1] Author's translation from the French.

The exchange of the notes herewith included regarding the establishment of diplomatic relations must take place before the expiration of the above-mentioned delay of forty-eight hours between the Ministers of Poland and Lithuania at Tallinn.

4. The above-mentioned proposal cannot be the object of a discussion either as regards contents or form—it is a proposition *ne varietur.*

Failure to reply or the proposal of any supplements or reservations whatever will be considered by the Polish Government as a refusal. In this negative case the Polish Government will guarantee the just interests of their State by measures of their own.

ANNEX TO THE NOTE [2]

Excellency, by order of my Government I have the honour to communicate the information that the Lithuanian Government have decided beginning from today to establish normal diplomatic relations between Lithuania and Poland and to this end establish a Legation at Warsaw. The duly accredited Lithuanian Minister will deliver his credentials at Warsaw by 31st March of the present year, at the latest.

The Lithuanian Government for their part guarantee to the Polish Legation at Kaunas the conditions for normal functioning and to this purpose will guarantee, beginning with the 31st of March of the present year, the possibility of direct communication by land, water, air, post, telegraph, and telephone between this Legation and the Polish Government.

[2] This Annex to the Note was signed upon instructions from the Lithuanian Government by the Lithuanian minister at Tallinn, Bronius Dailide, and delivered at the Polish Legation in Tallinn on March 19, 1938, at twelve noon, as demanded.

Appendix E

LITHUANIAN-RUSSIAN PACT FOR MUTUAL ASSISTANCE[1]

A treaty on the transfer of the city of Vilnius (Vilna) and the Vilnius region to the Republic of Lithuania and on mutual assistance between Lithuania and the USSR:

PRESIDENT OF THE REPUBLIC OF LITHUANIA on the one side and the SUPREME SOVIET OF THE USSR on the other side;

For the purpose of developing the friendly relations established by the peace treaty of July 12, 1920, and based on the recognition of an independent state existence and nonintervention in the internal affairs of the other party;

Recognizing that the peace treaty of July 12, 1920, and the pact on nonaggression and peaceful settlement of conflicts of September 28, 1926, continue to form a firm basis for their mutual relations and undertakings;

Convinced that a definition of the exact conditions insuring mutual security and a just settlement of the questions of State appurtenance of the city of Vilnius and the Vilnius region, unlawfully wrested from Lithuania by Poland, meet the interests of both contracting parties;

Found it necessary to conclude the following treaty on the transfer of the city of Vilnius and the Vilnius region to the Republic of Lithuania and on mutual assistance between the Soviet Union and Lithuania and appointed for this purpose their authorized representatives:

For the President of the Republic of Lithuania: Juozas Urbsys, Minister of Foreign Affairs; for the Presidium of the

[1] Author's translation from the Lithuanian.

Supreme Soviet of the USSR: Vyacheslaff Molotoff, Chairman of the Council of the People's Commissar of Foreign Affairs;

And these authorized representatives, on mutual presentation of their credentials, found in due form and good order, agreed on the following:

ARTICLE I

For the purpose of consolidation of friendly relations between Lithuania and the Soviet Union, the city of Vilnius and the Vilnius region are transferred by the Soviet Union to the Republic of Lithuania and included in the territory of the Lithuanian State, the boundary between the Soviet Union and the Republic of Lithuania being established in accordance with a map appended hereto, which boundary shall be specified in more detail in a supplementary protocol.

ARTICLE II

The Republic of Lithuania and the Soviet Union undertake to render each other every assistance, including military, in event of aggression or menace of aggression against Lithuania as well as in event of aggression or menace of aggression against the Soviet Union over Lithuanian territory on the part of any European power.

ARTICLE III

The Soviet Union undertakes to render the Lithuanian army assistance in armaments and other military equipment on favorable terms.

ARTICLE IV

The Republic of Lithuania and the Soviet Union undertake jointly to effect protection of the state boundaries of Lithuania, for which purpose the Soviet Union receives the right to maintain at its own expense, at points in the Republic of Lithuania established by mutual agreement, Soviet land and air armed forces of strictly limited strength. The exact location of these troops and the boundaries within which they may be quartered, their strength at each particular point, and also all other economic and administrative questions, questions of jurisdiction, and other questions arising in connection with the presence of Soviet armed forces on Lithuanian territory under the present treaty shall be regulated by special agreements. The sites and buildings necessary for this purpose shall be allotted by the Lithuanian Government on lease terms at a reasonable price.

ARTICLE V

In the event of menace of aggression against Lithuania or against the USSR over Lithuanian territory, the two contracting parties shall immediately discuss the resulting situation and take all measures found necessary by mutual agreement to secure the inviolability of the territories of the contracting parties.

ARTICLE VI

The two contracting parties undertake not to conclude any alliances or participate in any coalition directed against either of the contracting parties.

ARTICLE VII

Fulfillment of this treaty shall not affect in any way the sovereign rights of the contracting parties, in particular their state organization, economic and social systems, military measures, and generally the principle of nonintervention in internal affairs. The locations of the Soviet land and air armed forces (in Article III of this treaty) under all circumstances remain a component part of the territory of the Republic of Lithuania.

ARTICLE VIII

The term of validity of this treaty in regard to the undertakings for mutual assistance between the Republic of Lithuania and the USSR (Articles II and VII) is for fifteen years and unless one of the contracting parties finds it necessary to denounce the provisions of this treaty established for a specified term of one year prior to expiration of that term, these provisions shall automatically continue to be valid for the next ten years.

ARTICLE IX

This treaty comes into force upon exchange of instruments of ratification. Exchange of these instruments shall take place in Kaunas within six days from the day of signature of this treaty. This treaty is made in two originals, in the Lithuanian and the Russian language, at Moscow, October 10, 1939.

JUOZAS URBSYS
VYACHESLAFF MOLOTOFF

Appendix F

Foreign Exchange Quotations in Kaunas

DATE	NEW YORK	LONDON	BERLIN	PARIS	RIGA
	Litas to $1.00	*Litas to £1*	*Litas to 100 Rm.*	*Litas to 100 Frs.*	*Litas to 100 Lats*
Jan., 1928	10.06	49.00	240.00	39.41	194.45
Jan., 1929	10.07	48.80	239.69	39.53	194.00
Jan., 1930	10.00	48.74	238.90	39.34	193.07
Jan., 1931	10.01	48.60	238.11	39.27	192.80
Jan., 1932	10.02	35.16	238.91	39.51	189.00
Jan., 1933	10.04	33.74	238.54	39.25	.....
Jan., 1934	6.42	32.20	240.22	39.65	.....
Jan., 1935	5.99	29.24	240.00	39.37	.....
Jan., 1936	5.93	29.39	239.34	39.29	193.48
Jan., 1937	5.95	29.14	238.20	27.72	114.91
Jan., 1938	5.93	29.66	238.20	19.87	117.20
Jan., 1939	5.95	27.82	238.20	15.72	110.11
Oct., 1939	6.01	24.11	238.20	13.68	112.54

NOTE: The litas, the monetary unit of Lithuania, equals 100 centas and contains 0.150463 grams of fine gold. Its circulation in Lithuania was abolished by the Soviet government after the occupation in 1940.

BIBLIOGRAPHY

BIBLIOGRAPHY

PRIMARY SOURCES

Centraline Lietuvos Pieno Perdirbimo Bendroviu Sajunga—Pienocentras (The Central Union of Dairy Coöperative Societies of Lithuania—Pienocentras). Kaunas, 1938.

Centralinis Statistikos Biuras,[1] *The Lithuanian Government Statistical Almanac 1937*. Kaunas, 1938. Published in Lithuanian and in English.

—— *Lietuva Skaitmenimis, 1918–1928* (Lithuania in Figures, 1918–1928). Published in Lithuanian and in French.

—— *Lietuvos paseliu plotu ir gyvuliu surasymas 1935 m. birzelio 30 d.* (The Census of Crop Area and Livestock of Lithuania, June, 1935). Kaunas, 1935.

—— *Lietuvos Statistikos Metrastis* (Annual Statistics of Lithuania). Kaunas, Vol. I, 1924–26; Vol. II, 1927–28; Vol. III, 1929–30; annual 1931–39. Published in Lithuanian and in French.

—— *Lietuvos Uzsienio Prekyba* (Foreign Trade of Lithuania). Kaunas, annual 1930–38. Published in Lithuanian and in French.

—— *Statistikos Biuletenis* (Bulletin of Statistics). Kaunas, 1939.

League of Nations, *Monthly Bulletin of Statistics*. Geneva, 1938.

—— *Statistical Year-Book of the League of Nations*. For 1937–38, Geneva, 1938; for 1939–40, Geneva, 1940.

Lietuvos Bankas Bulletin. Volumes of 1932, 1938, and 1939. Kaunas.

Lietuvos Sutartys su Svetimomis Valstybemis (Treaties of Lith-

[1] The Central Bureau of Statistics, a Department of the Ministry of Finance of Lithuania.

uania with Foreign Countries). Published by the Ministry of Foreign Affairs under the direction of Pranas Dailide, Director of the Ministry of Foreign Affairs, Kaunas; Vol. I, 1919–29; Vol. II, 1929–39. Published in Lithuanian, in languages of other contracting parties, and in French.

Lietuvos Valstybes 1938 m. biudzetas su palyginamaisiais daviniais (The Lithuanian State Budget for 1938 with Comparative Data). Kaunas, 1938. Published in Lithuanian and in English.

Ministry of Finance, *Coöperation in Lithuania in 1932: Report of Inspection for Institutions and Establishments Having Public Accountancy.* Kaunas, 1934.

Salkauskas, K., *Lietuvos Novelos* (a collection of laws and decrees of Lithuania in force March 16, 1935, published in the Government Gazette Nos. 1–476). Kaunas, 1935.

Tautos Ukis (National Economy [weekly economic journal]). Volumes for 1935–39. Kaunas.

The Vilna Problem. Lithuanian Information Bureau, London, 1922. With five maps.

The Vilna Question (consultations of MM. A. DeLapradelle, Louis LeFur, and Andre N. Mandelstam concerning the binding force of the decision of the Conference of Ambassadors of March 15, 1923; authorized translation from the original texts). Hazell, Watson and Viney, Ltd., London, 1929.

SECONDARY SOURCES

Bass, John Foster, *The Peace Tangle.* Macmillan, New York, 1920.

Boerje, Colliander, *Die Beziehungen zwischen Litauen und Deutschland während der Okkupation 1915–1918.* Tidnings Och Tryckeri Aktiebolag, Abo, 1935.

Elsbergas, Stasys, *Lietuvos Zemes Reforma* (Land Reform in Lithuania). Kaunas, 1935.

Graham, Malbone W., *New Governments of Eastern Europe.* Holt, New York, 1927.

Ivinskis, Zenonas, "Krikscioniskosios Vakaru Europos santykiai su pagoniskaja Lietuva" (Relations between Christian Western Europe and Pagan Lithuania), Atheneum, Vol. IV, Kaunas, 1933.

—— "A Contribution to the History of the Conversion of Lithuania," *Baltic and Scandinavian Countries: a Survey of the Peoples and States on the Baltic with Special Regard to Their History, Geography, and Economics,* Vol. V, No. 1, Danzig, January, 1939.

Jasaitis, Antanas, *The History of the Lithuanian Nation and Its Present National Aspirations.* Lithuanian Catholic Truth Society, Philadelphia, 1919. 2d ed.

Kriksciunas, Jurgis, *Die litauische Landwirtschaft.* Verlag Zemes Ukio Rumai, Kaunas, 1933.

—— *Agriculture in Lithuania.* Lithuanian Chamber of Agriculture, Kaunas, 1938.

Kubilius, A. K., *Lietuvos Ukio Perspektyvos* (The Prospects of the National Economy of Lithuania). Kaunas, 1930.

League of Nations, *European Conference on Rural Life: 1939* (national monographs drawn up by various governments). *Lithuania,* Official Publication C. 28. m. 16, 1939, conf. E.V.R. 12, Geneva, April, 1939.

—— *Report of the Committee for the Study of the Problem of Raw Materials.* Geneva, 1937.

Lietukis, Lietuvos Zemes Ukio Kooperatyvu Sajunga, 1923–1933 (Lietukis, the Union of Agricultural Coöperative Societies, 1923–1933). Kaunas, 1933.

Losch, Otto, *Litauen, eine wirtschafts-geografische Darstellung.* "Juniores" Verlag, Königsberg, 1932.

Meyer, Herman, "*Die baltischen Staaten Estland, Lettland, Litauen,*" in *Ostsee Jahrbuch herausgegeben von der Industrie und Handelskammer zu Lubeck.* 1937.

Moravskis, A., *Lietuvos Finansai. Pinigai, kreditas ir bankai Lietuvoje pries kara ir dabar* (The Finance of Lithuania. Money, Credit and Banking in Lithuania before the War and at Present). II Dalis, Kaunas, 1925.

Moulton, Harold G., and Leo Pasvolsky, *War Debts and World Prosperity.* Brookings Institution, Washington, D.C., 1932.

Nauchno-Issledovatelskii Institut Monopolii Vneshnei Torgovli,

Torgovie otnoshenia SSSR s kapitalisticheskimi stranami (Trade Relations of USSR with Capitalistic Countries). Moskva, 1938.

Oberländer, Theodor, *Die landwirtschaftlichen Grundlagen des Landes Litauen.* Berlin, 1930.

Pfeitzner, Josef, *Groszfürst Witold von Litauen als Staatsman.* Verlag Rudolf M. Rohrer, Bruen, Prag, Leipzig, Wien, 1930.

Prapolianis, Kazys, *Lenku Apastalavimas Lietuvoje* (The Apostleship of Poles in Lithuania). Tevyne, New York, 1918.

Preston, T. H., *Economic Conditions in Lithuania.* Kaunas, November, 1935.

Royal Institute of International Affairs, *The Baltic States: a Survey of Political and Economic Structure and the Foreign Relations of Estonia, Latvia, and Lithuania.* Oxford University Press, 1938.

Salcius, Petras, *Kooperacija; Kooperacijos paskaitu kursas* (Cooperation; Lectures on Coöperation). Kaunas, 1931.

Sapoka, A., *Lietuvos Istorija,* Sv. Ministerijos K.L.K. Leidinys (History of Lithuania, the edition of the Publication Commission of the Ministry of Education). Kaunas, 1936.

Skalweit, B., *Die Landwirtschaft in den litauischen Gouvernements, ihre Grundlagen und Leistungen.* Jena, 1918.

Sruoga, Kazys, *Die Wirtschaft der Republik Litauen und ihre Notenemission.* Verlag der deutschen Buchhandlung, Kaunas, 1930.

Stakauskas, J., *Lietuva ir Vakaru Europa XIII amz.* (Lithuania and Western Europe in the 13th Century). Kaunas, 1934.

Stohr, Felix, *Die Wirtschaft der Republik Litauen in ersten Jahrzehnt ihres Bestehens 1918–1928.* Erlangen, 1930.

Ten Years of Lithuanian Economy. Report of the Chamber of Commerce, Industry, and Crafts, Kaunas, 1938.

Timoshenko, Vladimir P., *World Agriculture and the Depression* (Michigan Business Studies, Vol. V, No. 5). University of Michigan, Ann Arbor, 1933.

INDEX

INDEX

Bei Fragen zur Produktsicherheit wenden Sie sich bitte an:
If you have any questions regarding product safety,
please contact:

Walter de Gruyter GmbH
Genthiner Straße 13
10785 Berlin
productsafety@degruyterbrill.com